1

Table of Contents

INTRODUCTION

The SIFT exam, or "Selection Instrument for Flight Training" is utilized by the Army to determine if candidates are qualified for selection for flight officer training programs. The exam is designed to test multiple different aspects of potential candidates, which is intended to be predictors of training performance. Some of the sections might not seem to have anything to do with actual aviation, but another goal of the exam is to determine overall academic ability and essentially how hard you are willing to work for it or not. In short: how smart are you and do you possess the drive and motivation required to be a leader in the US Army.

Sections on the SIFT

There are 7 sections on the SIFT as follows:

1. Simple Drawings (SD) – 2 minutes, 100 questions
2. Hidden Figures (HF) – 5 minutes, 50 questions
3. Army Aviation Information Test (AAIT) – 30 minutes, 40 questions
4. Spatial Apperception Test (SAT) – 10 minutes, 25 questions
5. Reading Comprehension Test (RCT)– 30 minutes, 20 questions
6. Math Skills Test (MST) – 40 minutes, test length varies
7. Mechanical Comprehension Test (MCT) – 15 minutes, test length varies

From the time you check-in for the exam, count on the entire exam lasting approximately 3 hours, although many test-takers often complete the exam in about 2 hours. We will cover each section in detail in the following chapters of this book, each followed up with practice questions like those you will see on the SIFT exam.

Scoring on the SIFT

Scores range from 20-80 with a 40 being a passing score. The low 50's is an average score. Obviously, you want to try to do better than that since the selection process is a competitive one, although there is varied reports of whether or not boards actually see your score or just that you passed without indicator of actual score. Either way, you should not treat test-day as a "trial run" and study hard now. You are only allowed take the SIFT twice in your life!

Additional Test Information

The most important sections to study for are those that lend themselves to be studied. Kind of a confusing statement, right? What is meant by that is of the 7 sections, you should devote a majority of your study time to three of them: Math Skills, Mechanical Comprehension, and Army Aviation Information. These sections will have the most bang for your buck for study effort, especially since many test-takers probably haven't studied math or physics (as found in the Mechanical Comprehension section) for many years, and very possibly have zero real-world experience with aviation.

The other 4 sections (Simple Drawings, Hidden Figures, Spatial Apperception, and Reading Comprehension) you need to familiarize yourself with and move on, as these sections you cannot "study" much beyond that. Your objective in preparation for these sections is just to make sure the first time you see them isn't on test day.

Overall, you should only spend a few hours in combined total studying for Simple Drawings, Hidden Figures, Spatial Apperception, and Reading Comprehension. Many will find they only spend 1 or 2 hours on them...maybe even less. The rest of your time should be devoted to the other three sections as they are more substantially more difficult, more academically driven (as opposed to "skills" like the other sections), cover more material, and will result in higher scores for your study effort.

Additional Resources

Keep in mind that while the SIFT is a relatively new test (introduced in 2013), many of the sections were picked up from the AFOQT for the Air Force and ASTB for the Naval forces. While the number of questions and time limits are different, you can find a plethora of practice tests and helpful information on discussion forums online.

Be certain to visit www.usarec.army.mil and find your way to the SIFT FAQ's...or just Google "SIFT exam" or "SIFT FAQ" and it will be the very first result. This is the official information about the SIFT exam and you should read it carefully.

Testing Strategies

There are two very different strategies you will have to utilize on the SIFT exam as there are two different types of subtest sections you will encounter.

The first are the "fixed number of questions" sections: Simple Drawings, Hidden Figures, Army Aviation Information Test, Spatial Apperception, and Reading Comprehension. On these sections, any question left unanswered is counted as incorrect, which simply means, don't leave a single question unanswered! If you see time is running out, guess on every question before the clock runs down. Also on these sections, you can go skip questions or go back later, so if time permits, check your work before moving on.

The second type of subtest is the "Computer Adaptive" type. This is only for the Math Skills and Mechanical Comprehension. Under no circumstances should you ever guess without first giving your very best effort on these sections. The reasons are two-fold: 1) you cannot go back and change answers later. 2) the "Adaptive" word means that each test is customized to each test taker. As you answer questions, depending on whether or not you answer them correctly or not will determine the question you get next. If you get a question right, the next question will be more difficult. If you get it wrong, the next one will be easier. Each time you get a wrong answer, you maximum possible score drops lower and lower. Blindly guessing will significantly decrease the possibility of even passing this section, because after too many wrong answers you essentially fail automatically. This is why the test lengths vary, because if you get 5 or 10 questions in row correct, they know you are good to go and you can move on. If you miss 5 or 10 in a row, they know you don't have a prayer of passing so don't bother giving you any more chances.

Chapter 1: Simple Drawings

As indicated in the name, this section is simple. So simple in fact, you should not spend more than about 10 minutes "studying" for this section. No, we are not kidding. In fact, most people will only need about 90 seconds. In fact, it isn't even really possible to "study", but only familiarize yourself with how this test section is designed and what you need to do.

You will have a mere 120 seconds to answer 100 questions in which you select a shape or object that is not like the other shape or objects. The questions are so simple however, that a pre-kindergartner could answer them. No, again, we aren't kidding. A 3 or 4 year old could answer these questions....maybe not necessarily as quickly as you can, but the point remains. As you noticed though, the trick is not in the difficulty (or lack thereof) of the questions themselves, but the fact that no one can possibly answer all 100 in the short amount of time allotted: 1.2 seconds per question.

The best way to prepare for this section is to just run through some practice questions. We gave you a quarter of the actual test length to see what it is like. Get a stop-watch or pull up a timer on your phone and go through all 25 as fast as possible without sacrificing accuracy. This will give you a rough idea of how many questions you will be able to answer on the actual test. Once you've done that....move on to the other sections!

You can theoretically "guess" on this test section if time is running out, but we advise against it. The better strategy in this instance is to just answer as many correctly as possible. Let's say you have 10 seconds left on the clock. You could just click "A" for every answer as fast as possible and get through 10 or maybe even 15 of them if you are lucky. You have a 20% chance (1 in 5) of answering correctly, so you would have statistically answered 2 or 3 correctly. Most test-takers typically are able to answer in the range of 70-85 questions in the Simple Drawings section. That means on average, it takes them 1.4 to 1.7 seconds per question. That means in the remaining 10 seconds, most people will be able to correct answer 5 to 7 more questions.

The bottom line? Try it out now and time yourself so you know what to expect on test day and have a ballpark of your speed in questions/second. On test day, do not even look at the clock. Each glance at the clock could eat up another potentially answered question.

Simple Drawings Practice Test

1.
      □   □   □   □   ■

      A.   B.   C.   D.   E.

2.
      =   =   =   =   ⩾

      A.   B.   C.   D.   E.

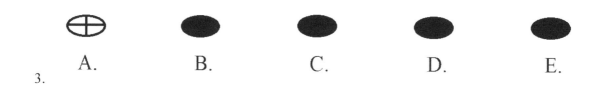

3.
      A.   B.   C.   D.   E.

4.
      ⇧   ⇧   ⇧   ⬆   ⇧

      A.   B.   C.   D.   E.

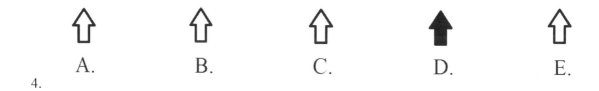

5.
      A.   B.   C.   D.   E.

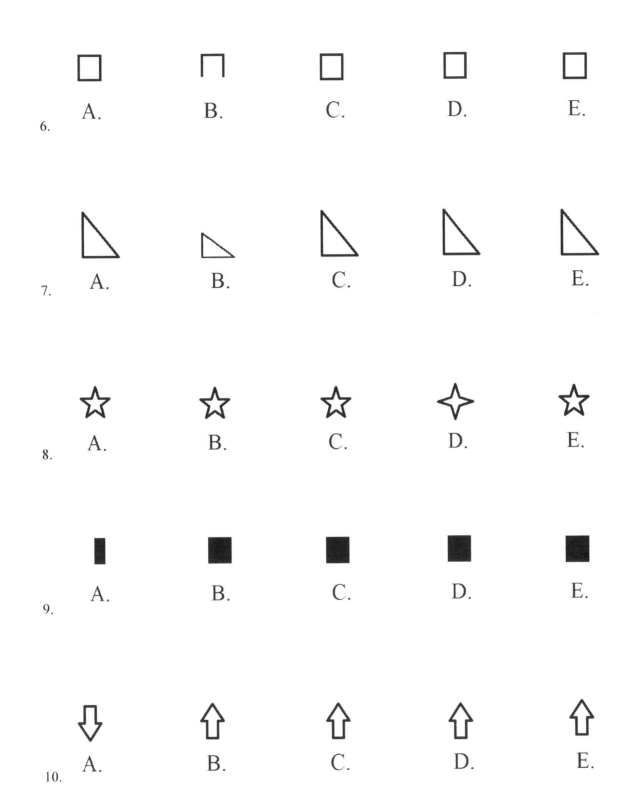

6.   A.   B.   C.   D.   E.

7.   A.   B.   C.   D.   E.

8.   A.   B.   C.   D.   E.

9.   A.   B.   C.   D.   E.

10.   A.   B.   C.   D.   E.

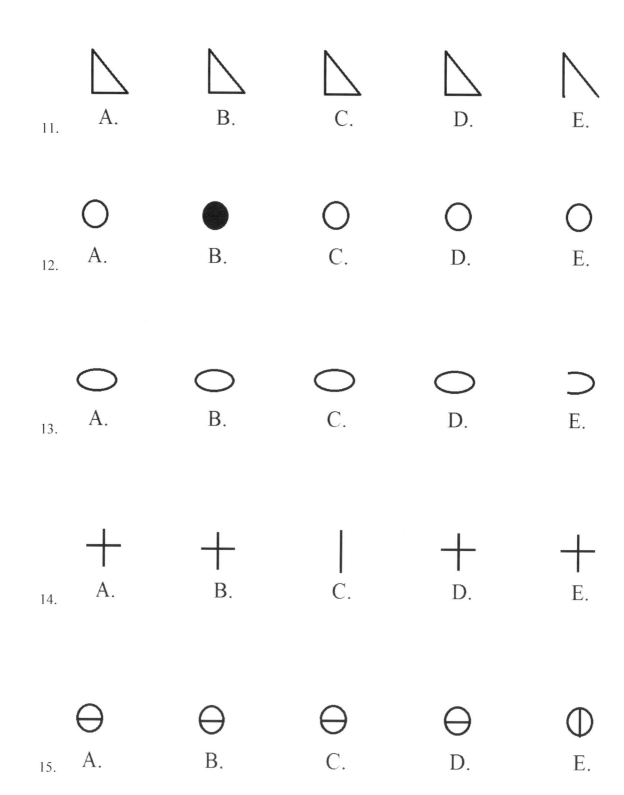

11. A.   B.   C.   D.   E.

12. A.   B.   C.   D.   E.

13. A.   B.   C.   D.   E.

14. A.   B.   C.   D.   E.

15. A.   B.   C.   D.   E.

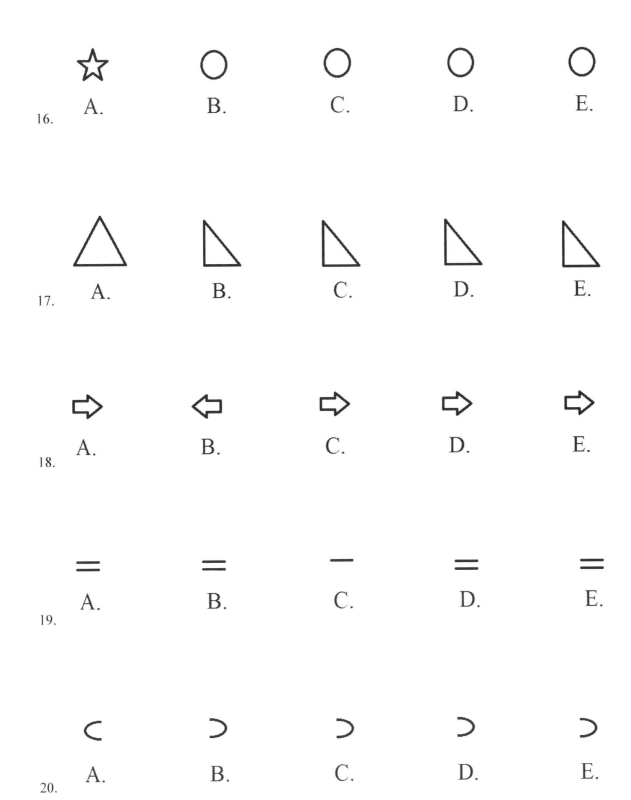

16. A. B. C. D. E.

17. A. B. C. D. E.

18. A. B. C. D. E.

19. A. B. C. D. E.

20. A. B. C. D. E.

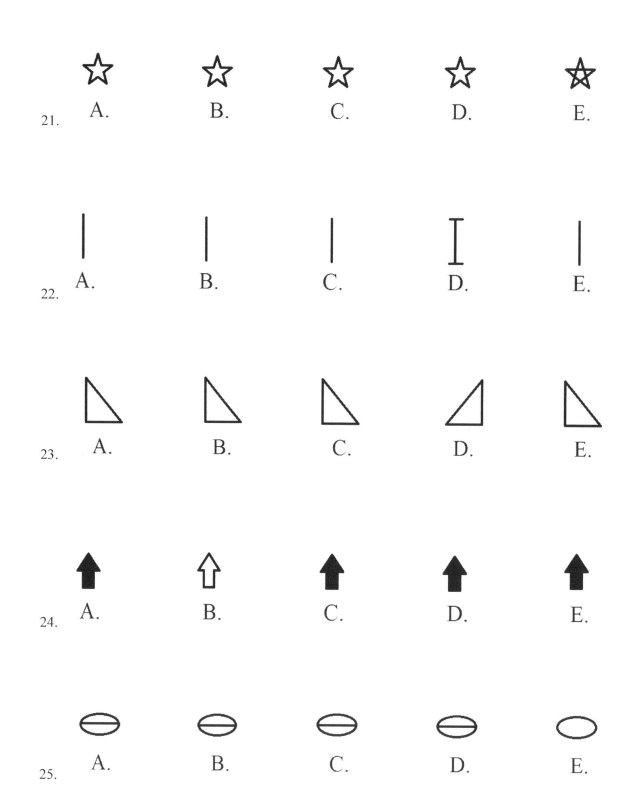

21.   A.   B.   C.   D.   E.

22.   A.   B.   C.   D.   E.

23.   A.   B.   C.   D.   E.

24.   A.   B.   C.   D.   E.

25.   A.   B.   C.   D.   E.

Simple Drawings – Answer Key

Do you *actually* need an answer key for this? If so, this could be a good opportunity to reconsider your career path…

Chapter 2: Hidden Figures

In the hidden figures section, you will have 5 minutes to complete 50 items. The first thing you will notice about this section is the formatting of the questions is totally different than any other section. You will be given 5 shapes with correlating answer choices A, B, C, D, & E. Below those answer choices, you will be presented the questions which is a box with a lot of zig-zagging lines in all directions. Somewhere in those zig-zagged lines is a shape that matches one of the 5 answer choices.

This section is straightforward enough, but a few things to remember that can help you:

- First and foremost, it is imperative to remember that the shape in the hidden figure will always match the same size, position, and orientation as shown in the answer choice selections. Do not over-analyze and think you see a figure that is rotated 90 degrees or slightly bigger or smaller because the SIFT will never present questions that way on this section.
- Find a defining feature of the answer choices. That one long section or sharply angled protrusion can help you quickly ID the shape in many cases.
- Speed is essential here. You have 6 seconds per question, so you need to move through the questions with a purpose and never linger on a question for too long. That said, don't rush because the objective is to answer the questions correctly, not to see how fast you can click.
- Finally, this works for some and not for others…but if you squint and almost blur out the hidden figure image a little, sometimes the shapes will just kind of "appear" because there is a pattern to them, whereas the other lines in the box are just meant to distract and conceal. Not very scientific, we know, but this has been a life-saver for many people.

Let's get started with some practice on the next page. Do not let the hidden figure section overwhelm you. Even if you are struggling with it, just get familiar with how this section looks so you know what to expect on test day, but focus your attention on the other sections as they are more important, require more study time, and you will see more results from your study effort.

For questions 1-5, use the below shapes as answer choices:

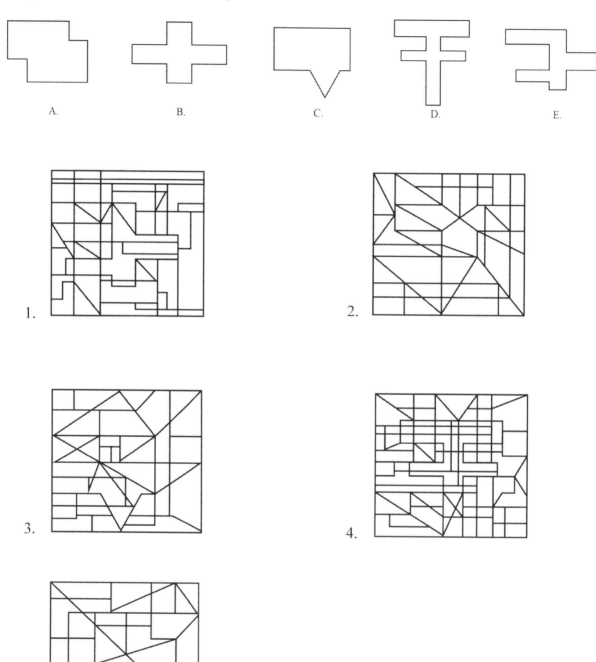

A.

B.

C.

D.

E.

1.

2.

3.

4.

5.

For questions 6-10, use the below shapes as answer choices:

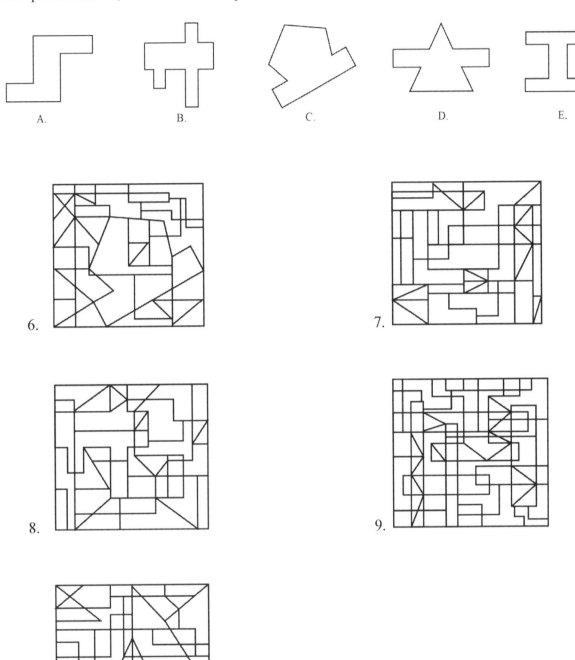

A.

B.

C.

D.

E.

6.

7.

8.

9.

10.

19

For questions 11-15, use the below shapes as answer choices:

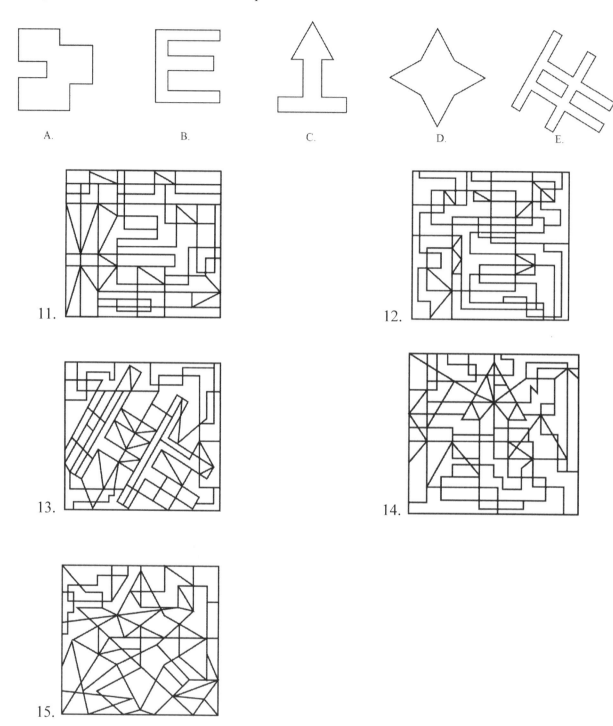

A.   B.   C.   D.   E.

11.

12.

13.

14.

15.

Hidden Figures Answer Key

1. E
2. B
3. C
4. D
5. A
6. C
7. A
8. B
9. E
10. D
11. A
12. B
13. E
14. C
15. D

Chapter 3: Army Aviation Information Test

The Army Aviation Information Test (AAIT) allows for 30 minutes to answer 40 multiple choice questions about aviation and helicopters in specific. If you have aviation experience such as private pilot's license, you are ahead of the curve but will still need to do some in depth studying as much of this information is technical and not so much about actually flying a plane. Unless you consider yourself an aviation expert already, you will need to study regardless of your current capability. Even those with PPL's report that this section was tough and required substantial studying effort.

A lot of information about helicopters is online. For example, the website of the Federal Aviation Administration (faa.gov) includes a 198-page, downloadable document, "Helicopter Flying Handbook." It is extremely important to download this resource and study it in depth. YouTube also has instructional videos about helicopters that can be quite helpful to better visualize and understand the concepts needed for this section.

Helicopter structure and components

During the past century, there have been many rotary-wing aircraft designed and built, including more than 400 types of helicopters. A helicopter is a type of rotorcraft that is able to takeoff and land vertically, hover, and fly forward, backward, and side to side (laterally). It can do so because it is equipped with a source of thrust: an engine that produces power and delivers it to overhead and tail rotors (on most helicopters) via one or more transmissions and drive shafts.

Helicopter engines are either piston or turbine; the advantage of the latter over the former is more thrust per pound.

Looking at a helicopter, we see a main body (fuselage) with a shaft (mast) protruding from the top. On the upper part of the fuselage of many helicopters is a cowling (shaped metal skin) that covers the aircraft's engine and transmission. Some helicopters have the engines externally mounted.

Depending on the type of helicopter, between two and six rotor blades are attached to the mast via a rotor head, which consists of several components, including a stabilizer bar (also called a flybar). The main rotor involves a complex swashplate mechanical system, which translate inputs from the pilot via the helicopter's flight controls into blade movement. Rotor system components include upper and lower swashplates, blade grips, control rods, pitch and scissor links, teeter or coning hinges, pitch horns, and counterweights.

The flybar's function is to enhance flight stability by keeping the bar stable as the rotor spins, and to reduce crosswind thrust on the blades. Through mechanical linkages, the bar's rotation combines with the swashplate's movement to damp internal (steering) and external (wind) forces on the rotor. The mechanical device makes it easier for the pilot to control the helicopter.

To provide additional stability, many helicopters have a horizontal stabilizer located roughly half way along the tail boom. The stabilizer helps to level the aircraft during forward flight.

Aft of the fuselage is a tail boom, which contains a drive shaft for the tail rotor, which is installed on the fin at the end of the helicopter. Tail rotors have two or more blades, depending on the size of the aircraft. They spin in the vertical plane, while the main, overhead rotor spins in an adjustable horizontal plane.

Some tail rotor tips are covered by a shroud made of formed metal or another durable material. The assembly is known as a ducted fan and the design reduces the possibility of someone walking into the spinning rotor blades and being injured or killed. The U.S. Coast Guard's Eurocopter HH-65 Dolphin is an example of a ducted fan helicopter.

Attached to the underside of many types of helicopters are a pair of skids that parallel the aircraft's longitudinal (nose-to-tail) axis. Some rotary-wing aircraft such as the U.S. Army's AH-64 Apache helicopter have wheels that hang down below the fuselage to absorb the weight of the aircraft when it is on the ground. Other helicopters have retractable wheels (called landing gear).

In a helicopter's cockpit are the pilots' seats, flight instruments and controls (cyclic, collective, throttle, and pedals), avionics (electronics used for navigation, communications, and aircraft systems), weapons controls (in military helicopters), and other equipment (e.g., fire extinguisher, flashlight).

Aerodynamics forces
There are four main aerodynamic forces that act on a helicopter when it is airborne: weight, lift, thrust, and drag.

Everything on a helicopter – the aircraft's structure and components, pilots, fuel, cargo, etc. – has *weight*. Because of the earth's gravitational pull, the combined mass of a helicopter and its contents acts downward. From a physics perspective, the total weight force is deemed to act through a helicopter's center of gravity.

Aerodynamic loads associated with flight maneuvers and air turbulence affect the aircraft's weight. Whenever a helicopter flies a curved flight path at a certain altitude, the load factor (force of gravity, or "G") exerted on the rotor blades is greater than the aircraft's total weight.

When a pilot turns a helicopter by banking it, the amount of "G" increases. Banking more in order to turn more tightly causes the aircraft's weight to increase further. A helicopter banked 30 degrees weighs an additional 16 percent, but at 60 degrees of bank – a very steep turn – the aircraft weighs twice as much as it does in straight and level flight in smooth air.

Gusts produced by turbulent air can suddenly increase the angle of attack (AOA) of the rotor blades, which enlarges the load factor acting on them.

Lift is the force that counteracts an aircraft's weight and causes a helicopter to rise into the air and stay aloft. Lift is produced by airfoils – rotor blades, in the case of helicopters – that move through the air at a speed sufficient to create a pressure differential between the two sides of the airfoils. Lift acts perpendicular to the direction of flight through the airfoil's center of pressure, or center of lift.

Thrust is an aircraft's forward force, which is created by one or more engines (there are three in some rotary-wing machines), and is transformed in the case of helicopters into rotary motion via the components mentioned (transmission, drive shafts, rotor head, blades). Generally, thrust acts parallel to the aircraft's longitudinal axis, but not always.

Drag opposes thrust; it is a rearward-acting force caused by airflow passing over the aircraft's structure and becoming disrupted. Drag acts parallel to the relative wind. There are three types of drag that act on aircraft: profile, induced, and parasite.

As the main and tail rotors spin and the helicopter accelerates, *profile drag* created by the blades' frictional resistance increases. Profile drag consists of skin friction created by surface imperfections and form drag; the latter is caused by wake turbulence, airflow separating from the surface of an aircraft structure and creating eddies. The amount of form drag is a function of the size and shape of the structure as it protrudes into the relative wind.

Induced drag is created by air circulating around each rotor blade as it spins and creates lift; the circulation causes a vortex behind each blade. There is also a downward deflection of the airstream. As more lift is produced, induced drag and rotor downwash both increase. As well, increasing the AOA of the rotor blades, a technique used to increase lift, results in stronger vortices and greater induced drag. Because helicopters need a lot of lift, particularly at low speeds and while hovering, a high AOA during takeoff and initial climb and final approach and landing results in the greatest induced drag. Conversely, at cruising airspeeds when the rotor blades' AOA is shallow, induced drag is relatively small.

Parasite drag is created by helicopter components and attached equipment that do not contribute to lift, including the fuselage and tail section, skids or wheels, externally mounted engines, sensors, and weapons. These structures create a loss of airstream momentum proportional to their size and greater parasite drag at higher airspeeds. In fact, parasite drag varies with the square of the aircraft's velocity, so doubling the airspeed quadruples this type of drag.

A helicopter's *total drag*, which can be plotted on a graph as a curve, with airspeed on the other axis, is the sum of its profile, induced, and parasite drag. The curve's low point is the intersection of a certain airspeed and the smallest total drag. In other words, it is the point where the helicopter's lift-to-drag ratio (L/DMAX) is the greatest. At this speed, the total lift capacity is maximized, an aspect of helicopter performance of singular importance to pilots.

Relevant scientific principles

Bernoulli's Principle

In 1738, a Swiss scientist named Daniel Bernoulli published a book entitled *Hydrodynamica* in which he explained that an increase of the inviscid flow of a fluid (i.e., the flow of an ideal, zero-viscosity liquid or gas) resulted in a decrease of fluid pressure. Bernoulli's famous equation is $P + \frac{1}{2}\rho v^2 = $ a constant, where P = pressure (a force exerted divided by the area exerted upon); ρ (the Greek letter "rho") = the fluid's density; and v = the fluid's velocity.

The constant in Bernoulli's formula is derived from the scientific principle that energy cannot be created or destroyed – only its form can be changed – and a system's total energy does not increase or decrease.

Conservation of energy

Bernoulli's Principle is based on the conservation of energy, which says that in a steady flow the sum of all forms of mechanical energy – a fluid's potential energy plus its kinetic energy – along a streamline (e.g., a tube) is the same at all points. Thus, greater fluid flow rate (higher speed) results in increased kinetic energy and dynamic pressure and reduced potential energy and static pressure.

A helicopter filled with fuel has a finite amount of energy. Through combustion in the engine, the fuel's heat energy is converted to kinetic energy through the transmission. If a helicopter were to be airborne when it ran out of fuel, the only energy left would be potential energy, a function of the aircraft's height above the ground. As the pilot nosed the helicopter down in order to keep air flowing over the rotor blades, a maneuver called autorotation, the aircraft's potential energy would be converted into kinetic energy.

Combining Bernoulli's Principle with the fact that helicopters have blades (airfoils) that spin and provide lift at varying speeds during different phases of flight (takeoff, climb, cruise, descent, landing), the lift produced in a given instant can be calculated using the following equation: $L = \frac{1}{2}\rho v^2 A C_l$, where L = the lift force, $\frac{1}{2}\rho v2$ was previously explained, A = the airfoil's area (length multiplied by width), and C_l is the coefficient of lift of the rotor blades.

Pilots must remember that the lifting force on their aircraft is proportional to the density (ρ) of air through which they fly (higher altitude = less dense air), the aircraft's speed, and airfoil AOA.

Venturi Effect
To understand how spinning rotor blades can produce enough force to lift a helicopter off the ground, climb, and maintain a cruising altitude, and how a moving tail rotor is able to generate a sideways, anti-torque force, we need to examine a phenomenon called the Venturi Effect.

In the late 18th century, an Italian physicist, Giovanni Battista Venturi, conducted experiments with a pump and an unusual tube. The diameter of one end of the tube was constant, while the circumference of the tube's central portion was smaller. Downstream from the bottleneck, the tube's diameter increased. It was as though someone had squeezed the center of the tube, creating a constriction.

Venturi noticed that as fluids moved through the tube, the flow rate increased (accelerated) and the force (static pressure) against the tube's surface decreased as the diameter became smaller. The opposite also happened: increasing tube diameter downstream resulted in reduced flow rate (deceleration) and greater static pressure. Venturi published his findings in 1797 and the effect that he observed, measured, and wrote about became associated with his name. It has certainly been integral to aviation since the development of gliding in the 19th century.

If a Venturi tube is cut in half longitudinally, the curvature of the tube wall would look similar to that of the top of a helicopter's rotor blade or an airplane's wing, which is also an airfoil. When a helicopter rotor blade spins, it "slices" the air, forcing molecules to travel along one side of the airfoil or the other. Those moving across the curved side have to travel a greater distance to reach the trailing edge than those moving across the relatively flat side. Consequently, the air molecules moving across the curved surface accelerate, as they did in Venturi's tube, and the static pressure drops.

Because pressure flows from high to low, the static pressure differential experienced between the two sides of rotating helicopter blades results in a force exerted on each airfoil from the high-pressure (flat) side to the low-pressure (curved) surface. In this way, lift is generated by the main rotor, and an anti-torque force acting perpendicular to the helicopter's longitudinal axis is created by the tail rotor (a smaller version of the overhead rotor turned vertically, essentially).

Newton's Third Law of Motion
Sir Isaac Newton (1642–1727) was a brilliant English physicist and mathematician who formulated universal laws of motion, including his third, which stated: "When one body exerts a force on a second body, the second body simultaneously exerts a force equal in magnitude and opposite in direction to that of the first body."

Rotor blades on helicopters designed and built in the United States, Canada, Britain, and Germany move in a counter-clockwise direction when viewed from above, and clockwise on rotary-wing aircraft made in Russia and other countries. Because of Newton's Third Law of Motion, the torque effect of the spinning main rotor is to rotate the aircraft in the opposite direction. To prevent this undesirable rotation, a sideways, anti-torque force is created on most helicopters by the spinning a tail rotor.

Alternatively, to eliminate torque counter-rotating rotors are used on other types of helicopters. Examples include the Boeing CH-47 Chinook (tandem rotors), Kaman K-1200 K-MAX (intermeshing rotors), and Kamov Ka-50 "Black Shark" (coaxial rotors).

Flight controls

As mentioned, a helicopter has four controls that allow the pilot to maneuver the aircraft: the cyclic, collective, throttle, and pedals.

The *cyclic* control, which is typically called the "cyclic" or "cyclic stick", is located in front of the pilot(s) in the cockpit. It is similar to a joystick used to play video games in that it moves in all directions except up and down. By moving the control, the pilot varies the pitch of the main rotor blades on a cyclical basis (i.e., every revolution) via the complex rotor head system. The rotor head has been designed so that all blades have the same angle of incidence (explained later) at the same point during each revolution (cycle).

Moving the cyclic results in a change of blade angle of attack, thus generating variable lift as each blade spins around the mast. Blades rise or fall in sequence due to increasing or decreasing AOA. For example, if the pilot moves the cyclic forward, the aft part of the rotor disk rises because of greater aft blade AOA, while the front drops. The result is a forward-tilting disk and a corresponding thrust vector imparted to the helicopter, which moves forward.

The *collective* is on the left side of the pilot's seat, moves up and down, and can be adjusted in terms of its position via a variable friction lock to prevent unwanted movement. Adjusting the collective alters the AOA of all the main rotor blades simultaneously, irrespective of their position. Pulling up on the collective increases blade AOA and aircraft climb rate; lowering it has the opposite effect.

In many helicopters, the *throttle*, which controls the power produced by the engine and rotates like a motorcycle throttle, is located at the end of the collective. In some turbine helicopters, the throttle control is mounted on the cockpit floor or an overhead panel. Single-engine helicopters typically have the motorcycle-style twist grip, while helicopters with two or more powerplants have a throttle lever for each engine.

Helicopter anti-torque *pedals* are located on the floor in front of the pilot(s) and used to control yaw (i.e., where the aircraft is pointing). Stepping on the left or right pedal causes the AOA of the tail rotor blades to change accordingly, altering the horizontal thrust vector created by the aft spinning airfoils. Viewed from above, the amount of horizontal "lift" (the sideways-acting force) generated by the tail rotor increases or decreases with pedal movement, changing the turning moment (force) acting on the helicopter in opposition to the torque force previously explained. As the tail moves left or right, the aircraft's nose moves in the opposite direction. When the pilot wants the helicopter's nose to move left or right, he or she pushes on the corresponding pedal.

Additional helicopter terms, definitions, and explanations (in alphabetical order)

Advancing blade: As the main rotor spins, with each revolution the blades move either toward the front of the helicopter or its tail. In the case of the former, each blade advances, and doing so increases the relative wind speed across the airfoil. Consequently, lift increases and the blade moves (flaps) upward.

Airflow in forward flight: When a helicopter flies forward, air flows in a direction opposite to that of the aircraft, with a speed equal to the machine's forward velocity. Because the rotor spins, the speed of air flowing across each blade depends on the airfoil's position in the plane of rotation and the helicopter's airspeed. With each revolution, the longitudinal velocity vector of each blade is sometimes with the aircraft's forward speed and sometimes against it.

Consequently, the airflow meeting each blade varies as a function of its position in the circular movement cycle. For helicopters with a main rotor that spins counter-clockwise, the maximum airflow speed happens when the blade reaches the three o'clock (right) position. As the blade passes over the aircraft's forward fuselage and nose, the speed decreases. The lowest airflow velocity happens when the blade reaches the nine o'clock (left) position. As the blade crosses the helicopter's tail, airflow speed increases to rotor spin (rotational) velocity and then accelerates as the blade moves toward the right side.

Airfoil: An airfoil is a surface that generates lift greater than drag as air flows over the upper and lower surfaces. Helicopter main rotor and tail rotor blades are examples of airfoils, as is the horizontal stabilizer. Airfoils are carefully designed and can be made of non-metallic materials such as composites.

Angle of attack: The angle between the chord line of an airfoil (e.g., a rotor blade) and the airfoil's direction of motion relative to the air (the relative wind). AOA is an aerodynamic angle.

Angle of incidence: The angle between the chord line of each blade and the rotor system's plane of rotation (e.g., level, tilted). AOI is a mechanical angle.

Autorotation: A situation where the main rotor generates lift not because of a functioning engine, but solely because air flows across the blades is called autorotation. When a helicopter engine fails, a clutch mechanism called a freewheeling unit automatically disconnects the engine from the main rotor, allowing the latter to spin freely. During autorotation, the helicopter descends, causing air to flow across the blades and continuing to provide lift as they spin in the airstream.

Learning to perform an autorotation to a successful landing is an important part of helicopter pilot training and must be demonstrated to an inspector in order to obtain the desired certification. To be certified with civil or military aviation authorities, helicopters must have a freewheeling unit that allows for autorotation.

Autorotation (during forward flight): During an autorotation when the helicopter is moving forward, the rotor disk takes in upward flowing air and the driven, driving, and stall regions of each blade move outboard along its length (span), but only on the retreating side of the disk. With a lower AOA on the advancing blade, the driven region expands, while on the retreating blade, the stall region enlarges. Also, reversed airflow occurs in a small section near the root of the retreating blade, reducing the driven region.

Autorotation (while hovering): During an autorotation in a hover (in still air), dissymmetry of lift due to helicopter speed is not a factor because the forces that cause the blades to spin are similar for all the airfoils, regardless of whether they are advancing or retreating. The force vectors acting in the driven, driving, and stall regions of each blade are different because the rotational relative wind is slower near the blade root and greater toward the blade tip. Also, there is a smaller AOA in the driven region compared to the driving region due to blade twist. Inflow of air up through the rotor combined with the rotational relative wind creates varying aerodynamic forces at every point along the blade.

In the driven region during an autorotation while hovering, some lift is produced, but it is offset by drag due to the total aerodynamic force (TAF) acting aft of the axis of rotation. The net result is rotor deceleration. The size of the driven region varies with the number of rotor revolutions per minute (rpm), blade pitch, and the rate of descent.

TAF in the driving region – also called the autorotative region – is angled slightly forward of the axis of rotation, resulting in an acceleration force that provides thrust and a blade rotation acceleration tendency. Rotor rpm, blade pitch, and rate of descent affect the driving region's size, which the pilot can control, thereby altering autorotative rpm.

The inner one-quarter of the rotor blade is the stall region and operates above the stall angle (the maximum AOA) during an autorotation while hovering. In this part of the rotor disk, drag is created that reduces blade rotation.

Blade flapping: Too much lift causes blade flapping. In a hover, the blade angle is such that lift and centrifugal forces balance out. However, if lift is increased (due to excessive airspeed of the advancing blades) and centrifugal force remains unchanged, the extra lift will cause the blade to move upward to a point where the lift and centrifugal forces are again in balance.

Blade span: The distance from the tip of the rotor blade to the center of the drive shaft (rotational center point).

Blade twist: Greater pitch angles toward the blade root where rotational velocity is relatively low and progressively shallower pitch angles toward the blade tip where rotational velocity is comparatively high describes the design feature known as blade twist. Its purpose is to distribute the lifting force more evenly along the airfoil, thereby smoothing out internal blade stresses.

Chord: The distance between the leading and trailing edges along the chord line is an airfoil's chord. If the blade is tapered, as viewed from above or below, the chord at its tip will be different than at its root. Average chord describes the average distance.

Chord line: An imaginary straight line from the airfoil's leading (front) edge to its trailing (aft) edge.

Coning: A spinning rotor creates centrifugal force (inertia) that pulls the blades outward from the hub. The inertia is proportional to the rotational speed. As the rotating blades produce lift – during takeoff, for example – centrifugal force combines with the upward lift force to create a slightly conical shape (when the rotor is viewed from the side).

Coning angle: The angle formed between spinning rotor blades and a plane perpendicular to the mast.

Coriolis Effect (Law of Conservation of Angular Momentum): The Coriolis Effect states that a rotating body spins at the same speed (angular momentum) unless an external force is applied to change the rotational velocity. Angular momentum is the rotational speed multiplied by the moment of inertia (mass times distance from the center of rotation squared). Also, angular acceleration and deceleration occurs as a spinning body's mass is moved closer to or farther away from the axis of rotation, respectively. The speed of the rotating mass changes proportionately with the square of the radius (the distance between the spinning body and the center of rotation).

In the context of helicopters, as coning occurs the rotor's diameter decreases. However, due to the law of conservation of angular momentum the blades' speed remains the same despite the fact that the tips now travel a shorter distance due to the smaller disk diameter. What changes is rotor rpm, which increases lift slightly.

Dissymmetry of lift: Different wind flow speeds across the advancing and retreating halves of the rotor disk result in a dissymmetry of lift. After a helicopter takes off, the relative wind speed experienced by the advancing blade is increased by the aircraft's forward speed, while the opposite occurs on the retreating blade (due to the machine's forward vector). Consequently, the advancing side of the rotor disk produces more lift than the retreating blade side.

Left uncorrected, this situation would cause the helicopter to become uncontrollable. To eliminate dissymmetry of lift, the main rotor blades flap and rotate automatically with each revolution. A semi-rigid rotor system (comprised of two blades, as is common on light helicopters) involves a teetering hinge, which allows the blades to flap as a unit; when one blade flaps down, the other blade flaps up. Rotor systems with three or more blades use a horizontal flapping hinge, which permits each blade to flap up and down as it rotates around the mast.

Driven region: Also called the propeller region, the driven region is nearest to the blade tips and normally consists of nearly one-third (30 percent) of the radius. The driven region tends to slow the rotor's spin due to drag resulting from the region's TAF, which is inclined slightly behind the axis of rotation.

Driving region: Also known as the autorotative region, the driving region is normally between a blade's driven and stall regions. The total aerodynamic force of the driving region is inclined slightly forward of the axis of rotation, supplying thrust and accelerating the blade's rotation.

Effective translational lift (ETL): Helicopters experience effective translational lift while transitioning to forward flight at about 16 to 24 knots. By the upper end of the speed range, the aircraft has managed to out-run the blade vortices created during takeoff and initial forward acceleration. During ETL, the rotor system begins to pass through air that is relatively undisturbed and the airflow becomes more horizontal, resulting in less downwash and induced drag. Also, efficiency of the rotor system and helicopter airspeed both increase during ETL and the machine accelerates toward the part of flight where L/DMAX occurs.

As the airspeed increases and translational lift becomes more effective, the aircraft's nose pitches up and the helicopter rolls to the right (with a rotor system spinning counter-clockwise), movements that must be corrected by the pilot. The machine's tendency to behave this way during ETL is the result of dissymmetry of lift, gyroscopic precession, and transverse flow effect. Once the helicopter has transitioned through ETL, the pilot must push forward and left on the cyclic to maintain a constant attitude of the rotor disk.

Forward flight: In steady forward flight, lift is offset by weight and the forces of thrust and drag are equal. When the tip-path (rotation) plane is tilted forward (due to the pilot pushing the cyclic forward), the total lift-thrust force, which consists of horizontal and vertical components, is also angled forward. Because of these horizontal components, as the helicopter moves forward it begins to lose altitude (due to the reduced vertical lift vector), a situation the pilot must correct.

As the helicopter begins to accelerate from a hover, translational lift causes the efficiency of the rotor system to increase, resulting in power in excess of that which was needed for hovering. Continued acceleration increases airflow and expands the excess power. Once the helicopter has reached its assigned or desired altitude and airspeed, the pilot reduces the power to maintain straight-and-level, unaccelerated flight, noting the torque (power) setting and not making any major changes to the flight controls.

Gyroscopic precession: When a force is applied to a spinning mass (e.g., a child's top, a helicopter rotor), the resulting effect occurs not at the point of force application, but 90 degrees later in the direction of rotation. In a helicopter, if a downward force is applied, say, on the starboard (right) side of the counter-clockwise-spinning rotor disk, the movement response occurs at the rotor's twelve o'clock position (i.e., in front of the fuselage). Wind gusts can apply such forces on rotors.

Hovering flight: One element of vertical flight is hovering. To hover a helicopter, the main rotor must produce lift equal to the aircraft's total weight. At high rotor rpm and increasing blade pitch (AOA) generate the lift required to hover. During hovering, rotor blade tip vortices reduce the effectiveness of the outer blade and negatively affect the lift of the following blades. For this reason, a lot of power is required during a hover.

Because of the helicopter's blade downwash (induced flow) while it is hovering, the velocity of air under the aircraft can reach 60 to 100 knots, depending on the rotor's diameter and the machine's size and weight.

During the hover, the relative wind and AOA are changed by the downward airflow and the TAF is reduced. Consequently, the pilot has to increase collective pitch (pull up on the collective) to create enough TAF to continue hovering. However, the increase in lift is accompanied by greater induced drag, so the total power needed to hover is greater, requiring the pilot to increase the engine throttle.

Induced flow (downwash): As rotor blades spin, they create rotational relative wind, airflow that is parallel as well as opposite to the rotor's plane of rotation and perpendicular to each blade's leading edge. As the blades rotate, air accelerates over the airfoils and is projected downward. Moving a large amount of air vertically and down through the rotor system, which occurs during takeoff and hover, creates induced flow, which can greatly alter the efficiency of the system. Rotational relative wind combines with downwash to form a resultant relative wind, which becomes more vertical as induced flow increases.

In ground effect (IGE): A "cushion" of air beneath moving airfoils (e.g., spinning rotor blades) and the takeoff/landing surface (e.g., a heliport deck) provides additional lift to the aircraft when it is close to the ground. During IGE, lift acts more vertically, induced drag is reduced, and the relative wind is more horizontal, all of which increases the efficiency of the rotor system. Maximum ground effect occurs during a hover above smooth, hard surfaces, up to a height equal to the main rotor's diameter.

Inherent sideslip: In forward flight, the tail rotor creates a sideward force and the helicopter slightly tilts to the wind when the main rotor disk is level and the slip ball in the pilot's turn-and-bank indicator is centered. The fin (vertical stabilizer) on larger helicopters is designed with the tail rotor mounted in such a way as to correct inherent sideslip. Also, installing the tail rotor on top of the fin places the anti-torque force vector closer to the horizontal plane of the main rotor's torque, reducing tilt when the aircraft is airborne.

Mean camber line: An imaginary line between the leading and trailing edges and halfway between the airfoil's upper (curved) and lower (relatively flat) surfaces.

Non-symmetrical airfoil (cambered): When one surface of an airfoil has a specific curvature that the opposite side does not, the airfoil is described as non-symmetrical, or cambered. The advantage of a non-symmetrical helicopter blade, for example, is that it produces lift at an AOA of zero degrees (as long as airflow is moving past the blade). Moreover, the lift-to-drag ratio and stall characteristics of a cambered airfoil are better than those of a symmetrical airfoil. Its disadvantages are center of the pressure movement chord-wise by as much as one-fifth the chord line distance, which causes undesirable blade torsion, and greater airfoil production costs.

Out of ground effect (OGE): Once a helicopter climbs to an altitude that exceeds the diameter of the main rotor, it is said to be out of ground effect. The IGE air "cushion" is gone and because the horizontal component of the relative wind decreases while induced drag increases, there is a decrease in lift. A greater blade angle is needed to maintain lift, but increasing the blade pitch also creates more drag. For this reason, increasing pitch while hovering in OGE requires more power than during an IGE hover. Also, under certain conditions there is a localized downward airflow that causes the helicopter to sink at an alarming rate, an effect called settling with power.

Pendular action: In terms of physics, a helicopter with a single main rotor is suspended from a single point in space and swings like a pendulum. Since a pilot can exacerbate pendular action by over-controlling the aircraft, he or she needs to fly using smooth control inputs.

Rearward flight: When the rotor disc is tilted rearward, flight in that direction occurs. In such a situation, the pilot must be mindful that the vertical component of the drag vector acts in the same direction as lift (up) and weight (down). Because the horizontal stabilizer on the tail boom is designed to function during forward, not rearward flight, when the latter occurs the likelihood of the tail skid striking the ground (at a very low altitude) increases. Also, with the pilot seated facing forward and the helicopter's skids (if so equipped) not curved upward on the aft end, rearward flight hazards are greater than when flying forward.

Relative wind: The flow of air in relation to a helicopter's blades is called the relative wind. It moves in a direction opposite to that of the aircraft and spinning rotor. Rotating helicopter blades experience a relative wind comprised of horizontal and vertical parts, the former resulting from the turning blades plus the aircraft's movement through the air, and the latter due to induced flow plus air movement as the helicopter climbs or descends.

Resultant relative wind: Airflow created by the rotor's spin and modified by induced flow (downwash) creates the resultant relative wind. When the helicopter is moving horizontally, the resultant relative wind changes with the aircraft's speed. The airspeed component of the relative wind is added to the rotational relative wind when the blade is advancing, and subtracted when the blade is retreating.

Retreating blade stall: As the helicopter's forward speed increases, the airspeed of the retreating blade decreases. However, to ensure aircraft flight stability the retreating blade needs to produce as much lift as the advancing blade. Therefore, the AOA of the retreating blade must be increased to augment lift in the retreating portion of the rotor disk. If the helicopter's forward speed reaches a value that exceeds the velocity associated with the maximum AOA of the retreating blade, it will stall (i.e., no longer generate lift).

When a rotor blade enters a stall, the pilot feels an abnormal vibration due to the loss of lift. A deepening stall results in the aircraft rolling and pitching nose up.

A blade stall is caused by high blade loading (due to high helicopter gross weight), low rotor rpm, operating at a high density altitude, steep or abrupt turns, and/or turbulent air.

With the onset of rotor blade stall, corrective action taken by the pilot involves reducing power (by lowering the collective), airspeed, and "G" loads during maneuvering; increasing rotor rpm to the maximum permitted; and checking pedal trim.

Rotational relative wind (tip-path plane): As rotor blades spin, they produce a rotational relative wind, as called tip-path plane. Rotational relative wind, which strikes a blade perpendicular to its leading edge and parallel to the plane of rotation, constantly changes as the rotor spins. The wind velocity is greatest at the tip of each blade and decreases to zero at the mast's center.

Rotor blade angles: Two rotor blade angles are key aspects of helicopter aerodynamics: angle of attack and angle of incidence.

Rotor system: A helicopter's rotor system consists of the following main components:

- Hub: the mechanical apparatus on the upper mast where the root of each rotor blade is installed.
- Tip: the rotor blade section farthest from the hub.
- Root: the part of the blade where it is attached to the hub.
- Twist: the change in angle designed and built into the blade from the root to the tip.

Settling with power: Also known as vortex ring state, settling with power occurs when a helicopter sinks into its own downwash. Settling with power involves a descent straight down or nearly vertical at a minimum of 300 feet per minute and low forward speed. As well, the main rotor system must be using between 20 and 100 percent of engine power, leaving – in some cases – insufficient power for the pilot to stop the sink rate.

Vortex ring state can occur during approaches with a tailwind or when there is turbulence caused by one or more nearby helicopters, as has happened during formation approaches.

Settling with power also creates a secondary vortex ring around each blade's point where airflow changes from up to down. The net result is turbulence over a considerable portion of the spinning blades, which causes a reduction of rotor efficiency despite the fact that the engine is still delivering power to the system.

Sideward flight: For a helicopter to fly sideways, the main rotor disc must be tilted in the desired direction, causing a sideways component of the lift vector to be generated and take effect on the aircraft. Because of parasite drag caused by the helicopter moving sideways through the air and the lack of a horizontal stabilizer for such movement, sideward flight can create a very unstable condition. The pilot needs to be aware of any obstruction to the left or right of the helicopter and bear in mind the relatively low position of the rotor disk edge at the three or nine o'clock position during sideward flight.

Stall region: The inboard one-quarter of the rotor blade is known as the stall region, which operates above the stall angle of attack and creates drag. The stall region tends to slow down the spinning rotor.

Symmetrical airfoil: When an airfoil has identical upper and lower surfaces, it is symmetrical and produces no lift at an AOA of zero degrees. The main rotor blades of most light helicopters are symmetrical.

Total aerodynamic force (TAF): Two components comprise the total aerodynamic force: lift and drag. The amount of lift and drag produced by an airfoil are primarily determined by its shape and area.

Translational lift: Enhanced rotor efficiency due to the helicopter transitioning from a hover to directional flight results in translational lift. The relative wind increases during directional flight acceleration, augmenting airflow across the rotor blades while the turbulence and vortices associated with hovering decrease.

Translating tendency (drift): A helicopter with one main rotor tends to drift in the direction of tail rotor thrust (i.e., laterally). The following features have been incorporated into helicopters (with a main rotor that spins counter-clockwise) to counteract the drifting tendency:

1. Tilting the rotor mast to the left (as viewed from behind the helicopter), which is accomplished by doing the same to the main transmission. The mast tilt opposes the tail rotor thrust responsible for the translating tendency.
2. Rigging the flight controls so that the main rotor disk is tilted slightly left when the cyclic is centered.

Translational thrust: While transitioning from hover to forward flight, relative wind flows across the tail rotor, increasing its aerodynamic efficiency, a phenomenon called translational thrust. As the tail rotor becomes more aerodynamically efficient, it produces greater anti-torque thrust, which results in the helicopter's nose yawing left (in a helicopter with a main rotor spinning counter-clockwise). To counteract the yaw, the pilot applies right pedal, decreasing the tail rotor blades' AOA.

Transverse flow effect: When accelerating in forward flight, induced flow (downwash) at the forward disk area decreases, while increasing in the aft disk area. The difference between the two rotor regions is called transverse flow effect. Because of the effect as well as gyroscopic precession, acceleration through about 20 knots or into a 20-knot headwind causes the helicopter (with a rotor that spins counter-clockwise) to roll to the right. Transverse flow effect is countered by the pilot moving the cyclic to the left.

Turning flight: In a banking turn, the rotor disk is tilted by movement of the cyclic to the left or right side, an action that creates a sideway component of the lift vector. This horizontal force – called the centripetal force – opposes inertia, or centrifugal force. As the bank angle increases, the centripetal force becomes greater, causing the turn rate to increase. However, the vertical component of the lift vector decreases. To compensate and maintain altitude, the pilot must enlarge the blades' AOA by increasing (pulling up on) the collective.

Vertical flight: To achieve vertical flight upward, the helicopter's lift and thrust must exceed its weight and drag. Increasing the main rotor blades' AOA while maintaining their rotational speed creates extra lift and the aircraft ascends. Decreasing the pitch results in a descent.

Vortex ring state: See *Settling with power*

1. A helicopter is:

    A. A type of gyrocraft.
    B. A type of rotorcraft.
    C. A category of rotary-wing airplanes.
    D. A sub-group of gyrocopters.

2. Helicopter turbine engines produce _____ thrust per pound than piston engines:

    A. less
    B. the same
    C. more
    D. the same, but only after factoring in the effect of density altitude

3. The main forces acting on a helicopter are:

    A. Induced lift, mass, thrust, and form drag.
    B. Lift, weight, thrust, and drag.
    C. Lift, gravity, air resistance, and rotor vortex drag.
    D. None of the above.

4. Helicopters typically have between __ and __ main rotor blade(s):

    A. 2, 6.
    B. 2, 10.
    C. 3, 8.
    D. 3, 7.

5. Depending on the type of helicopter, main rotor system components can include:

    A. A stabilizer bar, upper and lower swashplates, and counterweights.
    B. Pitch horns, teeter or coning hinges, and blade grips.
    C. Pitch and scissor links, and control rods.
    D. All of the above.

6. The function of the flybar is:

   A. To decrease crosswind thrust on the blades and enhance flight stability by keeping the bar stable as the rotor spins.
   B. To increase crosswind thrust and modify flight stability by allowing the bar to spin at a slower speed than the main rotor.
   C. To decrease crosswind thrust and augment flight stability by maintaining the bar at an acute angle to the main rotor.
   D. To spin in a direction opposite to the main rotor's, thereby reducing induced drag.

7. Many helicopters have a horizontal stabilizer located:

   A. On the mast.
   B. On the tail boom.
   C. On the fin.
   D. None of the above.

8. The purpose of the tail rotor is:

   A. To create kinetic energy that is transformed into potential energy as the helicopter climbs.
   B. To produce rotational momentum that is used by the transmission to drive a generator.
   C. To produce an anti-torque force acting perpendicular to the helicopter's longitudinal axis.
   D. All of the above.

9. Wheels on _____ types of helicopters are _____:

   A. all, retractable (to reduce drag).
   B. some, supplementary to skids.
     C. some, retractable.
   D. all, supplementary to skids.

10. A pilot controls a helicopter using:

    A. Flight instruments, hydraulic actuators, and a cyclic with a twist throttle.
    B. Flight instruments, pedals, two or more throttle levers, and avionics.
    C. Pedals, a throttle with a twist grip, collective link rods, and a cyclic.
    D. Pedals, and a collective, throttle, and cyclic.

11. From a physics perspective, the _____ force is deemed to act through a helicopter's
    _____:

    A. lift, center of motion.
    B. total weight, center of gravity.
    C. induced drag, longitudinal axis.
    D. total mass, center of motion.

12. When a pilot banks a helicopter, causing it to turn, _____:

    A. The machine's weight increases.
    B. The machine's weight remains the same.
    C. The machine's gravitational drag increases.
    D. The vertical component of the lift vector remains the same.

13. In the case of helicopters, lift is produced by _____ moving through the air at a
    speed sufficient to create _____:

    A. rotor blades, gyroscopic precession.
    B. the flybar, an anti-drag force.
    C. airfoils, a pressure differential.
    D. None of the above.

14. Thrust acts _____ to the aircraft's _____:

    A. at an acute angle, driven portion of the tail rotor disk.
    B. perpendicular, rotational relative wind.
    C. laterally, outer two-thirds of the main rotor disk.
    D. parallel, longitudinal axis.

15. Profile drag consists of _____ created by _____ and _____:

    A.   induced drag, angular momentum, aircraft components that do not contribute to lift.
    B.   skin friction, surface imperfections, form drag.
    C.   an inclined main rotor disk, increasing angle of attack, high blade rpm.
    D.   None of the above.

16. Vortices produced by spinning rotor blades create:

    A. Form drag.
    B. Rotational drag.
    C. Parasite drag.
    D. Induced drag.

17. When plotted on a graph, L/DMAX is the point where the helicopter's _____:

    A. Total lift-to-drag ratio is the greatest.
    B. Induced lift-to-drag ratio is maximized.
    C. Perpendicular lift component exceeds the rotational drag vector by at least 50 percent.
    D. Ability to carry pilots, cargo, etc. at the maneuvering speed is most fuel-efficient.

18. A helicopter's potential energy is affected by:

    A. The tail rotor's anti-torque force.
    B. The relative wind.
    C. The aircraft's height above the ground.
    D. All of the above.

19. Which of the following factors affect the lift produced by spinning rotor blades:

    A. Airfoil coefficient of lift.
    B. Air density.
    C. Blade area.
    D. All of the above.

20. What happens when a helicopter's main rotor blades spin rapidly?

    A. The angle of incidence decreases causing more lift on the retreating blades.
    B. The upper and lower sides of each blade experience a difference in pressure.
    C. Gyroscopic precession acts laterally on the aircraft.
    D. The center of pressure on each blade moves forward, creating a vortex.

21. Newton's Third Law of Motion applies to helicopters because:

    A. The spinning main rotor makes the aircraft try to spin in the opposite direction.
    B. Torque is balanced by the longitudinal drag vector.
    C. A ducted-fan helicopter produces less torque than an un-ducted one.
    D. Rotational relative wind opposes the angular momentum force.

22. When the pilot pushes the cyclic forward:

    A. The main rotor disk tilts forward.
    B. The blades' angle of attack on the rearward section of the tail rotor disk decreases.
    C. The angle of attack of the driven portion of the main rotor disk increases.
    D. All of the above.

23. Multi-engine helicopters have:

    A. A supplementary freewheeling clutch.
    B. A coaxial drive shaft and two transmissions.
    C. A throttle lever for each engine.
    D. All of the above.

24. When the pilot wants the helicopter's nose to move left or right, he or she:

    A. Pushes down on the collective for left motion and pulls up on it to turn right.
    B. Tilts the main rotor disk left or right while keeping the pedals neutral.
    C. Pushes on the left or right pedal while adjusting the cyclic to compensate for greater rotational drag.
    D. Pushes on the corresponding pedal.

25. For helicopters with a main rotor disk that spins counter-clockwise, the _____ airflow speed happens when each blade reaches the _____ position:

   A. median, nine o'clock (left)
   B. minimum, three o'clock (right)
   C. maximum, three o'clock (right)
   D. L/DMAX, six o'clock (aft)

26. On the advancing rotor blade, lift _____ and the blade _____:

   A. increases, angles up near the tip due to greater centripetal force.
   B. increases, moves upward.
   C. transitions outward, experiences stronger lateral torque.
   D. None of the above.

27. The angle between the _____ of a rotor blade and its direction of motion relative to the _____ is the angle of attack (AOA), which is _____ angle.:

   A. mean camber line, air, a constant.
   B. chord line, air, an aerodynamic.
   C. chord line, longitudinal airflow, a variable.
   D. mean camber line, longitudinal airflow, an acute.

28. The angle of incidence is between the _____ line of each blade and the rotor system's _____:

   A. mean chamber, forward-flight relative wind.
   B. mean chamber, rotational relative wind.
   C. chord, angular momentum.
   D. chord, plane of rotation.

29. When a helicopter engine _____, a clutch mechanism called a _____:

    A. fails; governing transmission is disconnected from the engine by the pilot, which allows the main rotor to spin freely.
    B. is shutdown after landing; gearbox controller is disconnected from the engine by the pilot, which allows the main and tail rotors to spin freely.
    C. accelerates too rapidly; terminal speed unit automatically disconnects the engine from the tail rotor, allowing it to spin freely.
    D. fails; freewheeling unit automatically disconnects the engine from the main rotor, allowing it to spin freely.

30. During an autorotation in forward flight, the rotor disk takes in _____ air and the driven, driving, and stall regions of each blade move _____ along its length (span), but only on the _____ side of the disk:

    A. upward flowing, outboard, retreating.
    B. downward flowing, inward, advancing.
    C. upward flowing, inward, retreating.
    D. ambient, outward, advancing.

31. Where there is too much lift, the main rotor blades will:

    A. Torque on the retreating blades.
    B. Twist.
    C. Flap.
    D. Create vortices in the driven region.

32. Centrifugal force _____ spinning helicopter main rotor blades _____.

    A. pushes, inward.
    B. pulls, outward.
    C. angles down, during autorotation.
    D. angles up, during liftoff.

33. If left uncorrected, greater lift produced by the advancing side of the rotor disk compared to the lift created by the disk's retreating side could make the helicopter _____:

A. fly in a sideslip.
B. vibrate excessively and come apart.
C. torque clockwise.
D. uncontrollable.

34. The driven region is _____ the blade tips and normally __ percent of the radius:

A. nearest, 30.
B. furthest from, 30.
C. mid-span from, 50.
D. nearest, 50.

35. The _____ region is normally between a blade's _____ and _____ regions:

A. stall, driven, high AOA.
B. stall, driving, low AOA.
C. driven, high AOA, stall.
D. driving, stall, driven.

36. Because of gyroscopic precession, if a wind gust applies a downward force on the left side of a helicopter's main rotor disk as it spins clockwise (as viewed from above), the movement response occurs at the __ o'clock position:

A. 9.
B. 6.
C. 12.
D. 3.

37. Helicopters experience effective translational lift while transitioning to forward flight at approximately __ to __ knots:

    A. 20, 28.
    B. 10, 20.
    C. 16, 24.
    D. 12, 24.

38. Maximum ground effect occurs during a hover up to a height equal to ___ percent of the main rotor's diameter:

    A. 50.
    B. 100.
    C. 150.
    D. None of the above.

39. A pilot can worsen a helicopter's pendular action by:

    A. Applying too much angle of incidence.
    B. Over-controlling the aircraft.
    C. Moving the cyclic left while pushing on the right pedal.
    D. Moving the cyclic left while pulling up on the collective.

40. The phenomenon of a helicopter sinking into its own downwash is called:

    A. L/Wmin (minimum lift-to-weight ratio).
    B. An airfoil stall.
    C. Vortex torque state.
    D. Settling with power.

Army Aviation Information Test – Answer Key

1. B
2. C
3. B
4. A
5. D
6. A
7. B
8. C
9. C
10. D
11. B
12. A
13. C
14. D
15. D
16. D
17. A
18. C
19. D
20. B

21. A
22. A
23. C
24. D
25. C
26. B
27. B
28. D
29. D
30. A
31. C
32. B
33. D
34. A
35. D
36. C
37. C
38. B
39. B
40. D

Chapter 4: Spatial Apperception

The Spatial Apperception section is simple, but deceiving. The best method to beating this section is to use a strategy for each and every question. Missed questions are 99% attributable to the test-taker looking at the question, abandoning their strategy because an answer "just looks right" at first glance. You will have 10 minutes to answer 25 questions, which is actually ample time once you get familiarized with the format.

First, let's review how the test is formatted. On the following page, you'll see there is an image of a horizon, typically with both water and land or some other distinguishable features to use as references. Imagine this is the view from the cockpit of an aircraft. Below this image, you will have 5 multiple choice options. Each option, A through E, shows the aircraft relative to the ground. Your task is to determine which aircraft represents the view from the cockpit.

The absolutely best strategy for this section is to employ a process of elimination and to follow that process strictly for each question. In each answer choice, the aircraft might be diving or climbing or flying level, banking left or right at various degrees or not banking at all, and traveling any direction (inbound, outbound, etc). It is best to start with the easiest and most obvious identifier, banking. For example, if you see that the image from the cockpit is flat and level, you can immediately remove any answer choice with any amount of bank either left or right which is represented by the horizon being tilted at an angle. If the horizon tilts UP to the right, the aircraft is banking right. If the horizon tilts UP to the left, the aircraft is banking left.

Next in the process of elimination, determine if the view from the cockpit is climbing or diving or level. This can be a little trickier because the differences are much more subtle and sometimes hard to distinguish. The best method is to find the vertical center-point of the view from the aircraft. If the horizon is ABOVE the centerpoint, the aircraft is diving. If it is BELOW the centerpoint, the aircraft is climbing. Remember, although it is more subtle than determining whether the aircraft is banking, this section is not intended to be devious such that you will have 5 answer choices of all aircraft in a dive but slightly more or less.

Finally, determine the orientation of the aircraft. For example, if the view from the cockpit shows water from edge to edge, you are obviously flying out to sea. So if there are answer choices showing the aircraft flying inbound to land or flying parallel to the coast, those are obviously incorrect.

This process of elimination can of course be modified for each test-taker. Some people find the orientation of the aircraft the most obvious and easy, so choose to start their process of elimination with that. Often, it is the diving and climbing that unnerves test-takers simply because they over-think it.

Here are some views from the aircraft with the attributable features:

Slight dive, no bank, & flying inbound to land (the "Land" is the dark area, the "water" is indicated with the little lines to represent waves). Notice the horizon is slightly above the center-point.

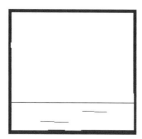

Climbing, no bank, & flying out to sea (note the horizon below the center-point)

Climbing, banking left, flying parallel to land (remember, the horizon slopes UP to the left, so the aircraft is banking left. The horizon is slightly below the center-point, so must be climbing).

Remember that with climbing and diving, the differences can be quite subtle. Do not overthink this! The answer choices are often quite different and by process of elimination, you will likely never encounter any problem where you have 2 or more answer choices that are too similar. Use the process of elimination and the correct answer will reveal itself.

Next, views of the aircraft with attributable features:

Aircraft flying flat and level, no bank

Aircraft flying at slight climb, banking left

Aircraft diving, no bank (possibly slight bank, but depends on viewpoint)

Aircraft climbing, banking left

Finally, let's look at an example problem and work through it step-by-step:

Remember, you can choose your own order of elimination, just start with whatever attribute is easiest for you to identify. In this case, let's start with direction of travel. In the view from the aircraft, it is obviously flying along the coastline. Therefore, answer choices B and E are immediately out because B is flying out to sea and E is flying inbound to land.

Next, still in terms of direction of travel, the land is on the left side of the image. Because of that, we know answer choice C must be incorrect as the view from the cockpit would have the land on the right side.

We are now down to only choices A and D remaining. As you can see from the view from the aircraft, the horizon is tilted, so we know the aircraft is banking. Without even worrying about what direction it is banking (FYI: it is banking left b/c the horizon slopes UP to the left), we know that answer choice A is incorrect because that aircraft is flat and level.

The only possible answer choice is D. You will note that we did not even get to whether the aircraft was in a climb or dive. In this case, the aircraft in answer choice D appears to be in a very slight climb. This helps illustrate the subtleness of the viewpoint from the cockpit. As you can see, the horizon is slightly below the center-point, although the land does climb slightly higher which can throw some people off. Typically, it's best to look at the water for a reference point since there are no variations in altitude.

Let's get started with the practice test. You will encounter 25 questions on the real test, for which you have 10 minutes to answer. That seems like a short time, but after the first couple of practice questions and get the feel for it, most people notice they can answer the questions easily in under 15-20 seconds. Again, once you get the hang of this section, move on to something else.

1.

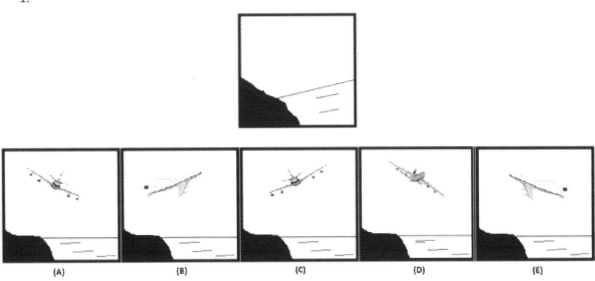

2.

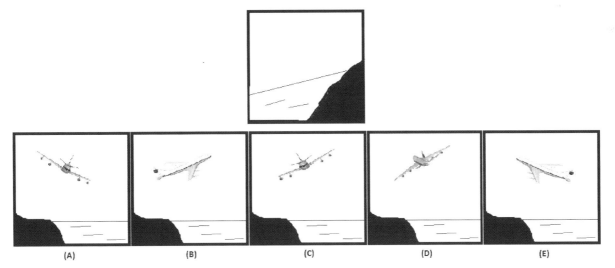

3.

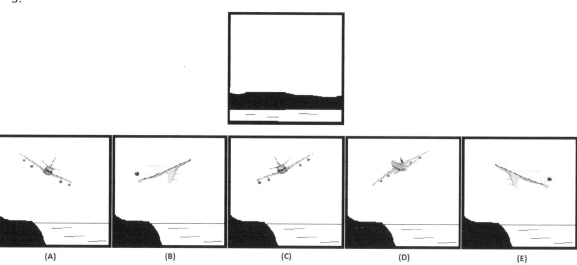

(A)   (B)   (C)   (D)   (E)

4.

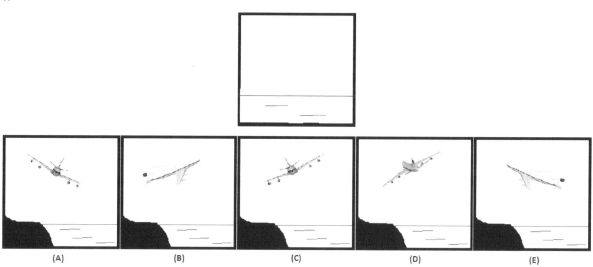

(A)   (B)   (C)   (D)   (E)

5.

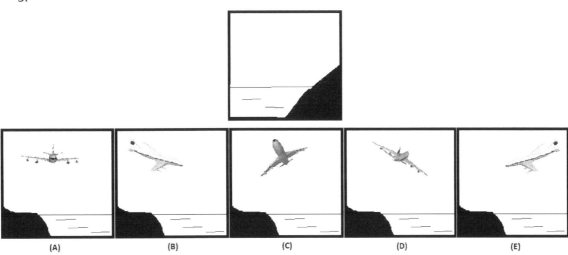

6.

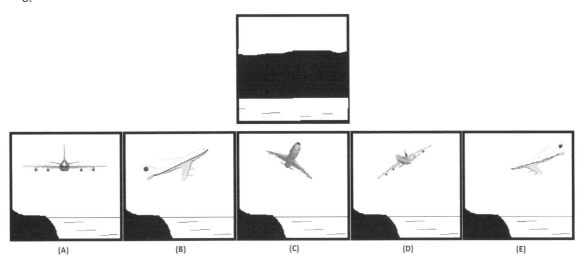

7.

(A)   (B)   (C)   (D)   (E)

8.

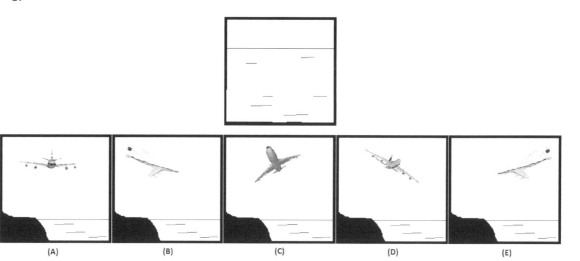

(A)   (B)   (C)   (D)   (E)

9.

(A)　(B)　(C)　(D)　(E)

10.

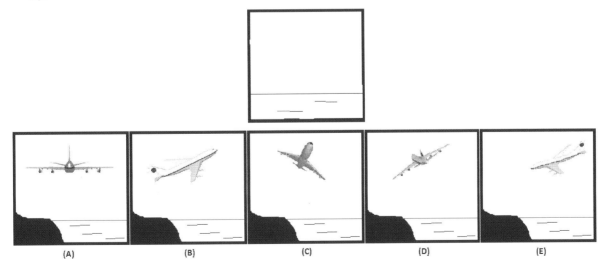

(A)　(B)　(C)　(D)　(E)

11.

(A)   (B)   (C)   (D)   (E)

12.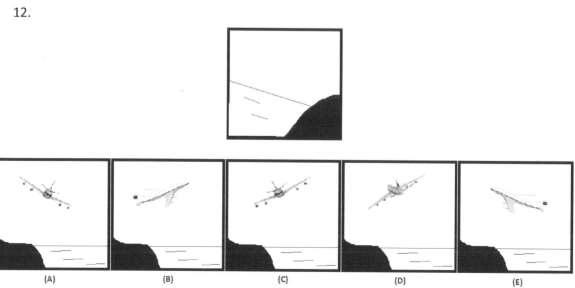

(A)   (B)   (C)   (D)   (E)

13.

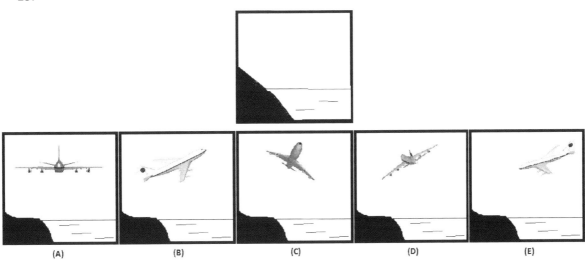

(A)   (B)   (C)   (D)   (E)

14.

(A)   (B)   (C)   (D)   (E)

15.

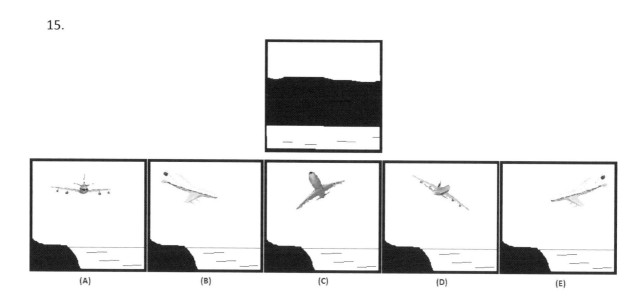

(A) (B) (C) (D) (E)

Spatial Apperception – Answer Key

1. D
2. C
3. E
4. B
5. A
6. E
7. C
8. B
9. D
10. B
11. C
12. A
13. A
14. D
15. E

Chapter 5: Reading Comprehension

The Reading Comprehension test measures your ability to understand, analyze, and evaluate written passages. You will be given 20 questions with a 30 minute time limit. The questions will generally be formatted such that you are presented a short passage and asked to find the answer choice that could have been inferred from only the information presented in the passage. The trick of this section is that many of the answer choices might be "true" or "feasible", but you will have to select the "best" answer.

We will cover the methods to best decipher and dissect the necessary information from a passage so that you can more quickly and accurately find the correct answer. After that, there are practice questions to help reinforce the review section so that the Reading Comprehension exam becomes relatively easy for you.

The Main Idea

Finding and understanding the main idea of a text is an essential reading skill. When you look past the facts and information and get to the heart of what the writer is trying to say, that's the **main idea**.

Imagine that you're at a friend's home for the evening:
>   "Here," he says, "Let's watch this movie."
>   "Sure," you reply. "What's it about?"

You'd like to know a little about what you'll be watching, but your question may not get you a satisfactory answer, because you've only asked about the subject of the film. The subject—what the movie is about—is only half the story. Think, for example, about all the alien invasion films ever been made. While these films may share the same general subject, what they have to say about the aliens or about humanity's theoretical response to invasion may be very different. Each film has different ideas it wants to convey about a subject, just as writers write because they have something they want to say about a particular subject. When you look beyond the facts and information to what the writer really wants to say about his or her subject, you're looking for the main idea.

One of the most common questions on reading comprehension exams is, "What is the main idea of this passage?" How would you answer this question for the paragraph below?

> "Wilma Rudolph, the crippled child who became an Olympic running champion, is an inspiration for us all. Born prematurely in 1940, Wilma spent her childhood battling illness, including measles, scarlet fever, chicken pox, pneumonia, and polio, a crippling disease which at that time had no cure. At the age of four, she was told she would never walk again. But Wilma and her family refused to give up. After years of special treatment and physical therapy, 12-year-old Wilma was able to walk normally again. But walking wasn't enough for Wilma, who was determined to be an athlete. Before long, her talent earned her a spot in the 1956 Olympics, where she earned a bronze medal. In the 1960 Olympics, the height of her career, she won three gold medals."

What is the main idea of this paragraph? You might be tempted to answer, "Wilma Rudolph" or "Wilma Rudolph's life." Yes, Wilma Rudolph's life is the **subject** of the passage—who or what the passage is about—but the subject is not necessarily the main idea. The **main idea** is what the writer wants to say about this subject. What is the main thing the writer says about Wilma's life?

Which of the following statements is the main idea of the paragraph?
   a) Wilma Rudolph was very sick as a child.
   b) Wilma Rudolph was an Olympic champion.
   c) Wilma Rudolph is someone to admire.

Main idea: The overall fact, feeling, or thought a writer wants to convey about his or her subject.

The best answer is **c)**: Wilma Rudolph is someone to admire. This is the idea the paragraph adds up to; it's what holds all of the information in the paragraph together. This example also shows two important characteristics of a main idea:

• It is **general** enough to encompass all of the ideas in the passage.

• It is an **assertion.** An assertion is a statement made by the writer.

The main idea of a passage must be general enough to encompass all of the ideas in the passage. It should be broad enough for all of the other sentences in that passage to fit underneath it, like people under an umbrella. Notice that the first two options, "Wilma Rudolph was very sick as a child" and "Wilma Rudolph was an Olympic champion", are too specific to be the main idea. They aren't broad enough to cover all of the ideas in the passage, because the passage talks about both her illnesses and her Olympic achievements. Only the third answer is general enough to be the main idea of the paragraph.

A main idea is also some kind of **assertion** about the subject. An assertion is a claim that something is true. Assertions can be facts or opinions, but in either case, an assertion should be supported by specific ideas, facts, and details. In other words, the main idea makes a general assertion that tells readers that something is true. The supporting sentences, on the other hand, show readers that this assertion is true by providing specific facts and details. For example, in the Wilma Rudolph paragraph, the writer makes a general assertion: "Wilma Rudolph, the crippled child who became an Olympic running champion, is an inspiration for us all." The other sentences offer specific facts and details that prove why Wilma Rudolph is an inspirational person.

Writers often state their main ideas in one or two sentences so that readers can have a very clear understanding about the main point of the passage. A sentence that expresses the main idea of a paragraph is called a **topic sentence.**

Notice, for example, how the first sentence in the Wilma Rudolph paragraph states the main idea:

"Wilma Rudolph, the crippled child who became an Olympic running champion, is an inspiration for us all."

This sentence is therefore the topic sentence for the paragraph. Topic sentences are often found at the beginning of paragraphs. Sometimes, though, writers begin with specific supporting ideas and lead up to the main idea, and in this case the topic sentence is often found at the end of the paragraph. Sometimes the topic sentence is even found somewhere in the middle, and other times there isn't a clear topic sentence at all—but that doesn't mean there isn't a main idea; the author has just chosen not to express it in a clear topic sentence. In this last case, you'll have to look carefully at the paragraph for clues about the main idea.

Main Ideas vs. Supporting Ideas

If you're not sure whether something is a main idea or a supporting idea, ask yourself the following question: is the sentence making a **general statement,** or is it providing **specific information?** In the Wilma Rudolph paragraph above, for example, all of the sentences except the first make specific statements. They are not general enough to serve as an umbrella or net for the whole paragraph.

Writers often provide clues that can help you distinguish between main ideas and their supporting ideas. Here are some of the most common words and phrases used to introduce specific examples:

1. **For example...**
2. **Specifically...**
3. **In addition...**
4. **Furthermore...**
5. **For instance...**
6. **Others...**
7. **In particular...**
8. **Some...**

These signal words tell you that a supporting fact or idea will follow. If you're having trouble finding the main idea of a paragraph, try eliminating sentences that begin with these phrases, because they will most likely be too specific to be a main ideas.

Implied Main Idea

When the main idea is implied, there's no topic sentence, which means that finding the main idea requires some detective work. But don't worry! You already know the importance of structure, word choice, style, and tone. Plus, you know how to read carefully to find clues, and you know that these clues will help you figure out the main idea.

For Example:

"One of my summer reading books was *The Windows of Time*. Though it's more than 100 pages long, I read it in one afternoon. I couldn't wait to see what happened to Evelyn, the main character. But by the time I got to the end, I wondered if I should have spent my afternoon doing something else. The ending was so awful that I completely forgot that I'd enjoyed most of the book."

There's no topic sentence here, but you should still be able to find the main idea. Look carefully at what the writer says and how she says it. What is she suggesting?
a) *The Windows of Time* is a terrific novel.
b) *The Windows of Time* is disappointing.
c) *The Windows of Time* is full of suspense.
d) *The Windows of Time* is a lousy novel.

The correct answer is **b)** – the novel is disappointing. How can you tell that this is the main idea? First, we can eliminate choice **c)**, because it's too specific to be a main idea. It deals only with one specific aspect of the novel (its suspense).

Sentences **a)**, **b)**, and **d)**, on the other hand, all express a larger idea – a general assertion about the quality of the novel. But only one of these statements can actually serve as a "net" for the whole paragraph. Notice that while the first few sentences praise the novel, the last two criticize it. Clearly, this is a mixed review.

Therefore, the best answer is **b)**. Sentence **a)** is too positive and doesn't account for the "awful" ending. Sentence **d)**, on the other hand, is too negative and doesn't account for the reader's sense of suspense and interest in the main character. But sentence **b)** allows for both positive and negative aspects – when a good thing turns bad, we often feel disappointed.

Now let's look at another example. Here, the word choice will be more important, so read carefully.

"Fortunately, none of Toby's friends had ever seen the apartment where Toby lived with his mother and sister. Sandwiched between two burnt-out buildings, his two-story apartment building was by far the ugliest one on the block. It was a real eyesore: peeling orange paint (orange!), broken windows, crooked steps, crooked everything. He could just imagine what his friends would say if they ever saw this poor excuse for a building."

Which of the following expresses the main idea of this paragraph?
a) Toby wishes he could move to a nicer building.
b) Toby wishes his dad still lived with them.
c) Toby is glad none of his friends know where he lives.
d) Toby is sad because he doesn't have any friends.

From the description, we can safely assume that Toby doesn't like his apartment building and wishes he could move to a nicer building **a)**. But that idea isn't general enough to cover the whole paragraph, because it's about his building.

Because the first sentence states that Toby has friends, the answer cannot be **d)**. We know that Toby lives only with his mother and little sister, so we might assume that he wishes his dad still lived with them, **b)**, but there's nothing in the paragraph to support that assumption, and this idea doesn't include the two main topics of the paragraph—Toby's building and Toby's friends.

What the paragraph adds up to is that Toby is terribly embarrassed about his building, and he's glad that none of his friends have seen it **c)**. This is the main idea. The paragraph opens with the word "fortunately," so we know that he thinks it's a good thing none of his friends have been to his house. Plus, notice how the building is described: "by far the ugliest on the block," which says a lot since it's stuck "between two burnt-out buildings." The writer calls it an "eyesore," and repeats "orange" with an exclamation point to emphasize how ugly the color is. Everything is "crooked" in this "poor excuse for a building." Toby is clearly ashamed of where he lives and worries about what his friends would think if they saw it.

Context Clues

Often in your reading you will come across words or phrases that are unfamiliar to you. How can you understand what you're reading if you don't know what all the words mean? You can often use **context** to determine meaning! That is, by looking carefully at the sentences and ideas surrounding an unfamiliar word, you can often figure out exactly what that word means.

For example, read the following paragraph:

> "Andy is the most unreasonable, pigheaded, subhuman life-form in the entire galaxy, and he makes me so angry I could scream! Of course, I love him like a brother. I sort of have to, because he *is* my brother. More than that, he's my twin! That's right. Andy and Amy (that's me) have the same curly hair and dark eyes. Yet though we look alike, we have very different dispositions. You could say that we're opposites. While I'm often quiet and pensive, Andy is loud and doesn't seem to stop to think about anything. Oh, and did I mention that he's the most stubborn person on the planet?"

As you read this passage, you probably came across at least two unfamiliar words: **dispositions** and **pensive**. While a dictionary would be helpful, you don't need to look up these words. The paragraph provides enough clues to help you figure out what these words mean.

Let's begin with **dispositions**. In what context is this word used? Let's take another look at the sentence in which it's used and the two sentences that follow: "Yet though we look alike, we have very different dispositions. You could say that we're opposites. While I'm often quiet and **pensive**, Andy is loud and doesn't seem to stop to think about anything."

The context here offers several important clues:

1. The sentence in which **dispositions** is used tells us something about what dispositions are not.

2. The sentence sets up a contrast between the ways that Amy and Andy look and between their dispositions; this means that dispositions are not something physical.

3. The general content of the paragraph. We can tell from the paragraph that dispositions have something to do with who Andy and Amy are, since the paragraph describes their personalities.

4. Yet another clue is what follows the sentence in which **dispositions** is used. Amy offers two specific examples of their dispositions: She's quiet and pensive, while Andy is loud and doesn't seem to think much.

These are specific examples of personality traits. By now you should have a pretty good idea of what the word dispositions means. A disposition is:
   a) A person's physical characteristics.
   b) A person's preferences.
   c) A person's natural qualities or tendencies.

The best answer, of course, is **c)**, a person's natural qualities or tendencies. While a person's disposition often helps determine his or her preferences, **b)**, this passage doesn't say anything about what Amy and Andy like to do (or not do). Nor are these characteristics physical, **a)**. Amy is talking about their personalities.

Now, let's look at the second vocabulary word: **pensive**. Again, the context provides us with strong clues. Amy states that she and Andy "are opposites" – that though they look alike, they have opposite dispositions; she is quiet, and he is loud. So we can expect that the next pair of descriptions will be opposites, too.

Now we simply have to look at her description of Andy and come up with its opposite. If Andy "doesn't seem to stop to think about anything," then we can assume that Amy spends a lot of time thinking.

We can therefore conclude that *pensive* means:
   a) Intelligent, wise.
   b) Deep in thought.
   c) Considerate of others.

The best answer is **b)**, deep in thought. If you spend a lot of time thinking, that may make you wise. But remember, we're looking for the opposite of Andy's characteristics, so neither **a)** nor **c)** can be the correct answer.

When you're trying to determine meaning from context on an exam, two strategies can help you find the best answer.

1. First, determine whether the vocabulary word is something positive or negative. If the word is something positive, then eliminate the answers that are negative, and vice versa.

2. Replace the vocabulary word with the remaining answers, one at a time. Does the answer make sense when you read the sentence? If not, you can eliminate that answer.

Cause and Effect

Understanding cause and effect is important for reading success. Every event has at least one cause (what made it happen) and at least one effect (the result of what happened). Some events have more than one cause, and some have more than one effect. An event is also often part of a chain of causes and effects. Causes and effects are usually signaled by important transitional words and phrases.

Words Indicating Cause: Because (of); Created (by); Caused (by); and Since.

Words Indicating Effect: As a result; Since; Consequently; So; Hence; and Therefore.

Sometimes, a writer will offer his or her opinion about why an event happened when the facts of the cause(s) aren't clear. Or a writer may predict what he or she thinks will happen because of a certain event (its effects). If this is the case, you need to consider how reasonable those opinions are. Are the writer's ideas logical? Does the writer offer support for the conclusions he or she offers?

Reading Between the Lines

Paying attention to word choice is particularly important when the main idea of a passage isn't clear. A writer's word choice doesn't just affect meaning; it also creates it. For example, look at the following description from a teacher's evaluation of a student applying to a special foreign language summer camp. There's no topic sentence, but if you use your powers of observation, you should be able to tell how the writer feels about her subject.

"As a student, Jane usually completes her work on time and checks it carefully. She speaks French well and is learning to speak with less of an American accent. She has often been a big help to other students who are just beginning to learn the language."

What message does this passage send about Jane? Is she the best French student the writer has ever had? Is she one of the worst, or is she just average? To answer these questions, you have to make an inference, and you must support your inference with specific observations. What makes you come to the conclusion that you come to?

The **diction** of the paragraph above reveals that this is a positive evaluation, but not a glowing recommendation.

Here are some of the specific observations you might have made to support this conclusion:

1. The writer uses the word "usually" in the first sentence. This means that Jane is good about meeting deadlines for work, but not great; she doesn't always hand in her work on time.

2. The first sentence also says that Jane checks her work carefully. While Jane may sometimes hand in work late, at least she always makes sure it's quality work. She's not sloppy.

3. The second sentence tells us she's "learning to speak with less of an American accent." This suggests that she has a strong accent and needs to improve in this area. It also suggests, though, that she is already making progress.

4. The third sentence tells us that she "often" helps "students who are just beginning to learn the language." From this we can conclude that Jane has indeed mastered the basics. Otherwise, how could she be a big help to students who are just starting to learn? By looking at the passage carefully, then, you can see how the writer feels about her subject.

Reading Comprehension Practice Test

Read each of the following paragraphs carefully and select the answer that can be inferred only from the information provided in the passage. You are to assume that all information presented in the passage is true and accurate for purposes of the exam. Some answer choices may be technically true or seem reasonable, but your only one choice can be derived only from the information presented.

REMEMBER: Pick the answer that ONLY contains information found in the passage. Do not use knowledge or information outside the text of each passage.

1. My "office" measures a whopping 5 x 7 feet. A large desk is squeezed into one corner, leaving just enough room for a rickety chair between the desk and the wall. Yellow paint is peeling off the walls in dirty chunks. The ceiling is barely six feet tall; it's like a hat that I wear all day long. The window, a single 2 x 2 pane, looks out onto a solid brick wall just two feet away.

   a) This office is small but comfortable.
   b) This office is in need of repair.
   c) This office is old and claustrophobic.
   d) None of the above.

2. There are many things you can do to make tax time easier. The single most important strategy is to keep accurate records. Keep all of your pay stubs, receipts, bank statements, and other relevant financial information in a neat, organized folder so that when you're ready to prepare your form, all of your paperwork is in one place. The second thing you can do is start early. Get your tax forms from the post office as soon as they are available and start calculating. This way, if you run into any problems, you have plenty of time to straighten them out. You can also save time by reading the directions carefully. This will prevent time-consuming errors. Finally, if your taxes are relatively simple (you don't have itemized deductions or special investments), use the shorter tax form. It's only one page, so if your records are in order, it can be completed in less than an hour.

   a) Simple strategies can make tax time less taxing.
   b) Don't procrastinate at tax time.
   c) Always keep good records.
   d) Get a tax attorney.

3. Being a secretary is a lot like being a parent. After a while, your boss becomes dependent upon you, just as a child is dependent upon his or her parents. Like a child who must ask permission before going out, you'll find your boss coming to you for permission, too. "Can I have a meeting on Tuesday at 3:30?" you might be asked, because you're the one who keeps track of your boss's schedule. You will also find yourself cleaning up after your boss a lot, tidying up papers and files the same way a parent tucks away a child's toys and clothes. And, like a parent protects his or her children from outside dangers, you will find yourself protecting your boss from certain "dangers"—unwanted callers, angry clients, and upset subordinates.

    a) Being a secretary is a lot like being a parent.
    b) After a while, your boss becomes dependent upon you, just as a child is dependent upon his or her parents.
    c) You will also find yourself cleaning up after your boss a lot, tidying up papers and files the same way a parent tucks away a child's toys and clothes.
    d) None of the above.

4. Day after day, Johnny chooses to sit at his computer instead of going outside with his friends. A few months ago, he'd get half a dozen phone calls from his friends every night. Now, he might get one or two a week. It used to be that his friends would come over two or three days a week after school. Now, he spends his afternoons alone with his computer.

    a) Johnny and his friends are all spending time with their computers instead of one another.
    b) Johnny's friends aren't very good friends.
    c) Johnny has alienated his friends by spending so much time on the computer.
    d) Johnny and his friends prefer to communicate by computer.

5. We've had Ginger since I was two years old. Every morning, she wakes me up by licking my cheek. That's her way of telling me she's hungry. When she wants attention, she'll weave in and out of my legs and meow until I pick her up and hold her. And I can always tell when Ginger wants to play. She'll bring me her toys and will keep dropping them (usually right on my homework!) until I stop what I'm doing and play with her for a while.

    a) I take excellent care of Ginger.
    b) Ginger is a demanding pet.
    c) Ginger and I have grown up together.
    d) Ginger is good at telling me what she wants.

6. The U.S is sending military aircraft with European and African Peacekeepers to help end the escalating conflict between Muslim militias and Christian rebel groups. According to the Pentagon, the U.S. military is assisting in this international peacekeeping mission to prevent, "a humanitarian and human rights catastrophe." The aircraft support is in response to France's request for "limited assistance."

   a) Intervention by an African Union-led force will be assisted by French Troops to protect civilians, stabilize the country and restore humanitarian aid.
   b) The United States of America is sending military aircraft to the African Union-led military in response to a request for assistance from France to help end a conflict between Muslim and Christian factions.
   c) Air transport assistance will help prevent sectarian violence from spreading further in this former French Colony.
   d) This conflict has already caused over 400,000 people to be displaced and if left unresolved it will result in a humanitarian and human rights catastrophe.

7. With the help of human genetic testing, we know more about our ancestors today than ever imaginable. An almost completed mitochondrial genome of an "early human-like species" has recently been reconstructed by scientists. The remains were found in an area of Northern Spain known as "The Pit of Bones." It is thought that this ancient relation to us was an ancestor to both "Neanderthals and the De nisovans." Researchers were surprised that the DNA (the oldest known to man) more closely resembled the De nisovans, not the Neanderthals, like expected. This 400,000 year old mystery will only be solved with more research.

   a) The oldest DNA is 400,000 years old and was found in an area of Southern Spain at a site called "the Pit of Bones." Researchers have been able to completely construct a full mitochondrial genome of this "early human-like species."
   b) The similarity in genetic code between this DNA sample and that of the Homo heidelbergensis is surprising since the only other known remains of the De nisovans were found in Siberia.
   c) The oldest know DNA was recently found in an area in Northern Spain.
   d) The DNA recently found in Northern Spain is a direct ancestor of our as shown in a completed mitochondrial genome, according to scientists.

8. The U.S. Patent and Trade Office received an interesting patent application on August 5, 2013 that could have profound implications for online companies such as Bitcoin. JPMorgan has successfully patented a "digital payment system… with new features that include a digital wallet and the ability to transfer money to anyone." They have also patented a payment software that will be completely anonymous and apparently "as easy as sending an email" to complete. This means that no one will have any way of knowing where the payment came from. This will provide a higher level of comfort and privacy for customers wish to make purchases through the internet.

    a) Bitcoin applied for two patents for digital payment software on August 5, 2013.

    b) JPMorgan's digital payment system provides features that are unlike anything else currently available on the internet and will provide more security as well as a smoother, quicker, transaction experience for its users.

    c) The payment software JPMorgan has patented is as easy as sending an email and will likely replace Bitcoin in the near future.

    d) Using the digital payment system that JPMorgan has now patented will provide a higher level of comfort and privacy for customers wishing to make a payment for purchases through the internet.

9. Most people in America pay for purchases using cash, debit, or credit card. The future of payments will include digital wallets and mobile payments using your mobile phone for many more Americans thanks to the trusted technology many of us already use today; Bluetooth. Although this technology is already available most people do not make use of this technology but combining this ability with the ease and comfort of the commonly known and used Bluetooth is expected to change our payment habits. The low power variant Bluetooth LE will not drain your phone's battery as with other similar, currently available technology.

    a) Although the technology to use digital wallets and mobile payments using your mobile phone is available, most Americans opt to pay for purchases using cash, debit, or credit card.

    b) Most people don't use newer technology to pay for purchases because these apps drain the battery on their mobile device far too quickly.

    c) Bluetooth is expected to change our payment habits.

    d) Many Americans already make use of Bluetooth technology with their mobile devices.

10. An area called Trinity Canyon in the state of Nevada was the chilly, isolated home for one family of 6 for two days. Four small children and both parents survived when their Jeep rolled and went down an embankment. Warming rocks in a fire and then bringing them inside the overturned vehicle not only prevented any of the 6 people from suffering frostbite, but kept the entire family warm while stranded in below freezing temperatures until they were finally found by three residents during a massive search effort. Experts say that making "all the right decisions" led to both to this family's survival and their high spirits when found.

   a) Lighting a fire and warming rocks inside the vehicle was the only reason this family of six survived two days in the subzero temperatures of Trinity Canyon.

   b) None of the 6 survivors of a car accident suffered from frostbite after spending two days in the chilly temperatures of the Trinity Canyon area of Nevada.

   c) Experts say that making "all the right decisions" may help increase your chances of surviving time in subzero temperatures for an extended amount of time.

   d) An area in the State of California was the chilly and isolated home for one family of 6 for two days.

11. The world recently said good-by to a "giant of history", Nelson Mandela in Johannesburg, South Africa. President Obama was joined by tens of thousands including royals, prime ministers, and ordinary South Africans to pay tribute to a man of whom the likes of, "we will never see the likes of…again" according to Obama. The celebration of Mandela's life took place in the same stadium that 23 years earlier he gave his first speech after his release from prison, and the place of his last public appearance at the World Cup final in July of 2010. Nelson Mandela would have found it fittingly ironic that this tribute to his life occurred on the same day as the United Nations' Human Rights Day.

   a) Nelson Mandela's memorial was purposely scheduled on the same day as the U.N's Human Rights Day to highlight Mandela's work to ending apartheid in South Africa.

   b) Tens of thousands joined in the four-hour celebration honoring the life of Nelson Mandela including royals, presidents, prime ministers and ordinary South Africans.

   c) Nelson Mandela will always be remembered by the world for his work with the anti-apartheid movement in South Africa.

   d) The stadium that held the memorial for Nelson Mandela was also the location of his last public appearance at the World Cup final in July of 2010.

12. General Motors Company made history recently when announcing that for the first time ever a female will head a major U.S. automaker. Mary Barra will take over from current CEO, Dan Akerson, in early 2014 according to company officials. GM made this important statement one day after the United States Treasury Department announced that it had sold its final financial stake in the company, therefore ending the 2009 bailout of the company. GM has bounced back from near bankruptcy since 2009 and has earned nearly $20 billion in net income since 2010, according to a recent CNN article.

a) Current General Motor's CEO, Dan Akerson, was voted out and will be replaced by Mary Barra in the early months of 2014, according to company officials.
b) GM only made this "first time in history" move after the U.S. Treasury Department announced that they no long owned any financial stake in the company.
c) General Motors has gone from near bankruptcy to profiting more than $20 billion in net income since the taxpayer bailout in 2009.
d) The U.S. Treasury Department announced that it will finally sell its remaining financial stake in GM early in the New Year.

13. Uruguay is in the position to become the first country in the world to have systems regulating the legal production, sale and consumption of marijuana, according to a recent CNN report. The only step that is left in the passing this law is for President Jose Mujica to sign the bill, but since he was publically known for supporting such legislation, it is being seen as a "done deal". CNN reports that this landmark piece of legislation places this South American country at the vanguard of liberal drug policies, even surpassing the Netherlands, where recreational drugs are illegal but a policy of tolerance is in place. Supporters of this bill are hoping that it will encourage other Latin American countries to adopt similar pieces of legislation.

a) Uruguay will be the first country in the world to legalize the production, sale, and consumption of marijuana once the legislation is signed by President Jose Mujica.
b) Only the Netherlands will be considered more liberal with their laws regarding the use of recreational drugs.
c) President Jose Mujica has not been known for supporting this piece of historic legislation and it is unknown if he will indeed sign the bill in the near future.
d) Once this bill is passed as law in Uruguay, it is assumed that other Latin American countries will adopt similar laws in their countries.

14. An article recently published in the Journal of the American Academy of Child and Adolescent Psychiatry states that there has been a 42% increase in the number of reported cases of ADHD since 2003 in children. The report goes on to state that today, 6.4 million between the ages of 4 and 17 have been diagnosed with ADHD, which is 2 million more than in 2007. Although this news is quite alarming, according to Dr. John Walkup, director of child and adolescent psychiatry at Weill Cornell Medical College and New York-Presbyterian Hospital, feels that there is also good news within this statistic. He feels that the increasing diagnosis rate of ADHD is getting closer to the actual number of children who are affected by ADHD; a number he feels is much higher than previous statistics indicate.

    a) An increase of 42% in the number of reported cases of ADHD since 2003 in children is an alarming and unexpected finding of recently completed research.

    b) Dr. John Walkup feels that the increase in the number of confirmed cases of ADHD means that it is a wider spread problem than statistics have indicated in the past.

    c) ADHD is becoming an epidemic in American children according to a recent report in the Journal of the American Academy of Child and Adolescent Psychiatry.

    d) More and more families are willing to have their children diagnosed with ADHD because the larger numbers indicate that it is becoming a more acceptably recognized disease across America.

15. Cyber bullying continues to be a growing problem across America. Reports can be found almost weekly of tweens and teens being bullied through social network sites and social applications. The concern is that these kids aren't using sites and apps that most of us are familiar with, such as Facebook and Twitter. According to a report recently found on CNN, free apps such as Ask.fm and Kik are the more commonly used tools of bullying. These sites are free and therefore anyone can create fake accounts and torment other children without facing any consequences or fear of retribution.

    a) New apps such as Ask.fm and Kik are the reason cyber bullying is continuing to grow as a problem in American schools.

    b) Since anyone can create fake accounts to bully other children with there is no way to stop this problem.

    c) Children and teens should not have use of mobile phones or computers. That would keep them safe from cyber bullying.

    d) Social networks and apps are the newest form of bullying; better known as cyber bullying.

16. NASA launched IRIS, a telescope that has taken amazing images of a layer of the sun's surface never previously seen before, according to scientists. IRIS, or, Interface Region Imaging Spectrograph, is collecting data from a little-known area of the sun that can be found between the solar surface and the outer atmosphere. Researchers are hoping that studying this area of the sun will answer some of this star's secrets such as the great fluctuation of temperature between the surface and the corona. To date, researchers are encouraged by findings being transmitted back from IRIS.

    a) The Interface Region Imaging Spectrograph is a NASA telescope sent into space to study a particular area of the sun's surface.

    b) Understanding the great fluctuations in temperature on the sun's surface is one of the key goals of this NASA mission into space.

    c) The photos that IRIS is sending back to NASA researchers will solve many of the sun's mysteries over the next few years.

    d) The data being collected by IRIS will be used by NASA for developing ways to harness the power of the sun as a renewable energy source here on Earth.

17. Canada and Russia are locked in a land dispute over the Arctic Circle. Canada's claims are based on an almost finished study of the arctic seabed and Russia is basing its claim on sheer presence as it continues to send more military personnel into the area. Canada is determined to assert and defend its claim to the Arctic but will continue to proceed through the appropriate science-based channels and in accordance to International Law. Russian President, Vladimir Putin has reportedly committed to "devote special attention to deploying infrastructure and military units in the Arctic" according to a Yahoo.com article. The ultimate answer of who owns the Arctic Circle will come from the UN's Commission on the Limits of the Continental Shelf.

    a) Russian President Vladimir Putin is relying on a combination of military persuasion and on-going scientific studies to prove that the Arctic Circle rightfully belongs to them.

    b) Canada intends to fully abide by International Law and finish scientific research to prove to the UN's Commission on the Limits of the Continental Shelf that the Arctic Circle legally is part of their land.

    c) This article is an example that both Russia and Canada are in a race to "claim the Arctic Circle" as their own land and will use tried but true methods to win this race.

    d) Being willing to devote special attention to deploying infrastructure and military units to the Arctic shows that Russia is invested in building this most remote area into usable land for its country.

18. Sedimentary deposits collected from the NASA's Mars rover Curiosity indicate that a lake existed that contained fresh-water and was likely able to support microbial life, according to geologist John Grotzinger, with the California Institute of Technology. Samples of clay drilled from rocks collected from an area known as Yellowknife Bay, indicates that this fresh-water lake existed when other areas of the planet were either dry or contained pools of water that were not life-sustaining. This news is significant because scientists are now able to develop a new strategy to looking for organics in other areas of this planet. This is opening a whole new world of research for scientists.

    a) Curiosity, NASA's Mars rover collected samples that proved that Mars had many lakes that were capable of supporting microbial life.

    b) NASA scientists are using the information gained by Curiosity to develop new strategies for gathering organics on other planets in our solar system.

    c) NASA has proven that there was once microbial life on Mars.

    d) Geologist John Grotzinger, with the California Institute of Technology has found supporting scientific proof that at one point in time Mars contained a fresh-water lake capable of supporting microbial life.

19. Three years of impasse and fiscal instability and potentially another partial government shutdown might all be ills thoughts of the past if a bipartisan budget deal is successful in the U.S. Congress. This potential history-making agreement is considered to be a "good first step" according to current President Obama and is being praised by the Republican leadership of the U.S. House of Representatives. If this budget deal is successful, it could be the beginning to a new era of cooperation in U.S. politics.

    a) A bipartisan budget deal could end three years of political impasse and fiscal instability if it passes in the U.S. Congress.

    b) President Obama hesitantly considered this agreement to be a "possibly tentative first step" towards a new era of cooperation in U.S. politics.

    c) Democratic leaders in the U.S. House of Representatives are praising this budget deal.

    d) If this agreement is not successful in the U.S. Congress, there will be another partial government shutdown early in 2014.

20. The Pentagon may be cutting out all U.S.-based commissaries in 2015 to help with a huge cost-saving effort, according to Fox News. These grocery stores that provide discounted food and other necessities not only to members of the military, but also to their families and veterans may be a thing of the past as Congress tries to trim its budget. According to the Defense Commissary Agency, more than 30% is saved on monthly grocery bills by shopping at one of the 178 commissaries found in the United States or any of the 70 found overseas. Not only would this discount be lost, if these commissaries closed, but over 30% of the employees at these stores are military spouses which would lead to wide-spread job loss for military families.

    a) To help trim the military budget, Congress plans to decrease the number of commissaries located in the U.S.A. as well as over-seas.

    b) If these stores close military personnel would not only lose out on savings of about 30% on their monthly bills, but many military families would lose one source of income for their families.

    c) Roughly 20% of commissaries' employees have a spouse serving in the military.

    d) The decision to close any or all 178 commissaries in the United States and over 70 over-seas is to be decided by the Defense Commissary Agency by 2015.

Reading Comprehension – Answers

1. c)
2. a)
3. a)
4. c)
5. d)
6. b)
7. c)
8. d)
9. a)
10. b)
11. d)
12. c)
13. a)
14. b)
15. d)
16. a)
17. b)
18. d)
19. a)
20. b)

Chapter 6: Mathematics Skills Test

The Math Skills Test section tests various concepts in numbers and operations, algebra, geometry, data analysis, statistics, and probability. In this test section, you will be provided 40 minutes to answer a varying number of questions. This is an adaptive test section, so the number of questions you answer depends on whether you answered previous questions correctly or not. Do NOT guess on questions unless you absolutely are stuck, and even then do your best to eliminate wrong choices first. Before taking the SIFT, you want to make sure that you have a good understanding of the math areas covered. You will need to sharpen your skills, but don't worry – we'll provide you with the knowledge that you'll need to know for the test. We have 70 practice questions, which is substantially more than you will encounter on the exam, but this will give you an opportunity to hone your skills on the different concepts. Remember to take your time, accuracy is paramount on the Math Skills Test since you cannot go back and change answers!

Math Concepts Tested

You have a much better chance of getting a good Math Knowledge score if you know what to expect. The test covers math up to and including the first semester of Algebra II as well as fundamental geometry. You will not be given any formulas, such as those required for geometry calculations, so you need to make sure that you have studied them so they are fresh in your mind.

Here is a breakdown of areas covered:

Numbers and Operations
Absolute values, inequalities, probabilities, exponents, and radicals.

Algebra and Functions
Basic equation solving, simultaneous equations, binomials & polynomials, and inequalities.

Geometry and Measurement
Angle relationships, area and perimeter of geometric shapes, and volume.

Math skills that you won't need:
- Working with bulky numbers or endless calculations.
- Working with imaginary numbers or the square roots of negative numbers.
- Trigonometry or calculus.

Important Note: You are not allowed to use a calculator for any section of the SIFT.

The Most Common Mistakes

Here is a list of the four most commonly- made mistakes concerning mathematics, starting with the most common.

1. Answer is the wrong sign (positive / negative).

2. Order of Operations not following when solving.

3. Misplaced decimal.

4. Solution is not what the question asked for.

These are the basics that individuals tend to overlook when they only have a minute or less to do their calculations. This is why it is so important that you pay attention right from the start of the problem. You may be thinking, "But, those are just common sense." Exactly! Remember, even simple mistakes still result in an incorrect answer.

Strategies

Review the Basics: First and foremost, practice your basic skills such as sign changes, order of operations, simplifying fractions, and equation manipulation. These are the skills you will use the most on almost every problem on the Math Knowledge and the Arithmetic tests sections. Remember when it comes right down to it, there are still only four math operations used to solve any math problem, which are adding, subtracting, multiplying and dividing; the only thing that changes is the order they are used to solve the problem.

Although accuracy counts more than speed; **Don't Waste Time** stuck on a question! Remember, you only have 40 minutes to answer 30 questions for this section test. This is why your knowledge of the basics is so important. If you have to stop and think about what 9 * 6 equals, or use your fingers to add 13 + 8, then you need to spend time on these fundamentals before going on to the concepts.

Make an Educated Guess: If necessary, eliminate at least one answer choice as most probably incorrect and guess which one is most likely correct from the remaining choices.

Math Formulas, Facts, and Terms that You Need to Know

The next few pages will cover the various math subjects (starting with the basics, but in no particular order) along with worked examples. Use this guide to determine the areas in which you need more review and work these areas first. You should take your time at first and let your brain recall the math necessary to solve the problems, using the examples given to remember these skills.

Order of Operations

PEMDAS – **P**arentheses/**E**xponents/**M**ultiply/**D**ivide/**A**dd/**S**ubtract

Perform the operations within parentheses first, and then any exponents. After those steps, perform all multiplication and division. (These are done from left to right, as they appear in the problem) Finally, do all required addition and subtraction, also from left to right as they appear in the problem.

Example: Solve $(-(2)^2 - (4 + 7))$.
$(-4 - 11) = -15$.

Example: Solve $((5)^2 \div 5 + 4 * 2)$.
$25 \div 5 + 4 * 2$.

$5 + 8 = 13$.

Positive & Negative Number Rules

$(+) + (-) =$ Subtract the two numbers. Solution gets the sign of the larger number.

$(-) + (-) =$ Negative number.

$(-) * (-) =$ Positive number.

$(-) * (+) =$ Negative number.

$(-) / (-) =$ Positive number.

$(-) / (+) =$ Negative number.

Greatest Common Factor (GCF)

The greatest factor that divides two numbers.

Example: The GCF of 24 and 18 is 6. 6 is the largest number, or greatest factor, that can divide both 24 and 18.

Geometric Sequence

Each term is equal to the previous term multiplied by *x*.

Example: 2, 4, 8, 16.

$x = 2$.

Fractions

Adding and subtracting fractions requires a common denominator.

Find a common denominator for:

$$\frac{2}{3} - \frac{1}{5}$$

$$\frac{2}{3} - \frac{1}{5} = \frac{2}{3}\left(\frac{5}{5}\right) - \frac{1}{5}\left(\frac{3}{3}\right) = \frac{10}{15} - \frac{3}{15} = \frac{7}{15}$$

To add mixed fractions, work first the whole numbers, and then the fractions.

$$2\frac{1}{4} + 1\frac{3}{4} = 3\frac{4}{4} = 4$$

To subtract mixed fractions, convert to single fractions by multiplying the whole number by the denominator and adding the numerator. Then work as above.

$$2\frac{1}{4} - 1\frac{3}{4} = \frac{9}{4} - \frac{7}{4} = \frac{2}{4} = \frac{1}{2}$$

To multiply fractions, convert any mixed fractions into single fractions and multiply across; reduce to lowest terms if needed.

$$2\frac{1}{4} * 1\frac{3}{4} = \frac{9}{4} * \frac{7}{4} = \frac{63}{16} = 3\frac{15}{16}$$

To divide fractions, convert any mixed fractions into single fractions, flip the second fraction, and then multiply across.

$$2\frac{1}{4} \div 1\frac{3}{4} = \frac{9}{4} \div \frac{7}{4} = \frac{9}{4} * \frac{4}{7} = \frac{36}{28} = 1\frac{8}{28} = 1\frac{2}{7}$$

Probabilities

A probability is found by dividing the number of desired outcomes by the number of possible outcomes. (The piece divided by the whole.)

Example: What is the probability of picking a blue marble if 3 of the 15 marbles are blue?

3/15 = 1/5. The probability is **1 in 5** that a blue marble is picked.

Prime Factorization

Expand to prime number factors.

Example: 104 = 2 * 2 * 2 * 13.

Absolute Value

The absolute value of a number is its distance from zero, not its value.

So in $|x| = a$, "x" will equal "$-a$" as well as "a."

Likewise, $|\,3\,| = 3$, and $|-3\,| = 3$.

Equations with absolute values will have two answers. Solve each absolute value possibility separately. All solutions must be checked into the original equation.

> **Example:** Solve for x:
> $|2x - 3| = x + 1$.
>
> Equation One: $2x - 3 = -(x + 1)$.
> $2x - 3 = -x - 1$.
> $3x = 2$.
> $x = 2/3$.
>
> Equation Two: $2x - 3 = x + 1$.
> $x = 4$.

Mean, Median, Mode

Mean is a math term for "average." Total all terms and divide by the number of terms.

> Find the mean of 24, 27, and 18.
> $24 + 27 + 18 = 69 \div 3 = 23$.

Median is the middle number of a given set, found after the numbers have all been put in numerical order. In the case of a set of even numbers, the middle two numbers are averaged.

> What is the median of 24, 27, and 18?
> 18, **24**, 27.
>
> What is the median of 24, 27, 18, and 19?
>
> 18, 19, 24, 27 ($19 + 24 = 43$. $43/2 = 21.5$).

Mode is the number which occurs most frequently within a given set.

> What is the mode of 2, 5, 4, 4, 3, 2, 8, 9, 2, 7, 2, and 2?
>
> The mode would be **2** because it appears the most within the set.

Exponent Rules

Rule	Example
$x^0 = 1$	$5^0 = 1$
$x^1 = x$	$5^1 = 5$
$x^a \cdot x^b = x^{a+b}$	$5^2 * 5^3 = 5^5$
$(xy)^a = x^a y^a$	$(5 * 6)^2 = 5^2 * 6^2 = 25 * 36$
$(x^a)^b = x^{ab}$	$(5^2)^3 = 5^6$
$(x/y)^a = x^a/y^a$	$(10/5)^2 = 10^2/5^2 = 100/25$
$x^a/y^b = x^{a-b}$	$5^4/5^3 = 5^1 = 5$ (remember $x \neq 0$)
$x^{1/a} = \sqrt[a]{x}$	$25^{1/2} = \sqrt[2]{25} = 5$
$x^{-a} = \dfrac{1}{x^a}$	$5^{-2} = \frac{1}{5^2} = \frac{1}{25}$ (remember $x \neq 0$)
$(-x)^a$ = positive number if "a" is even; negative number if "a" is odd.	

Roots

Root of a Product: $\sqrt[n]{a \cdot b} = \sqrt[n]{a} \cdot \sqrt[n]{b}$

Root of a Quotient: $\sqrt[n]{\dfrac{a}{b}} = \dfrac{\sqrt[n]{a}}{\sqrt[n]{b}}$

Fractional Exponent: $\sqrt[n]{a^m} = a^{m/n}$

Literal Equations

Equations with more than one variable. Solve in terms of one variable first.

Example: Solve for y: $4x + 3y = 3x + 2y$.

Step 1 – Combine like terms: $3y - 2y = 4x - 2x$.

Step 2 – Solve for y: $y = 2x$.

Inequalities

Inequalities are solved like linear and algebraic equations, except the sign must be reversed when dividing by a negative number.

Example: $-7x + 2 < 6 - 5x$.

Step 1 – Combine like terms: $-2x < 4$.

Step 2 – Solve for x. (Reverse the sign): $x > -2$.

Solving compound inequalities will give you two answers.

Example: $-4 \leq 2x - 2 \leq 6$.

Step 1 – Add 2 to each term to isolate x: $-2 \leq 2x \leq 8$.

Step 2: Divide by 2: $-1 \leq x \leq 4$.

Solution set is **[-1, 4]**.

Algebraic Equations

When simplifying or solving algebraic equations, you need to be able to utilize all math rules: exponents, roots, negatives, order of operations, etc.

1. Add & Subtract: Only the coefficients of like terms.

   Example: $5xy + 7y + 2yz + 11xy - 5yz = 16xy + 7y - 3yz$.

2. Multiplication: First the coefficients then the variables.

   Example: Monomial * Monomial.

   $(3x^4y^2z)(2y^4z^5) = 6x^4y^6z^6$.

   (A variable with no exponent has an implied exponent of 1.)

   Example: Monomial * Polynomial.

   $(2y^2)(y^3 + 2xy^2z + 4z) = 2y^5 + 4xy^4z + 8y^2z$.

   Example: Binomial * Binomial.

   $(5x + 2)(3x + 3)$.

91

First: $5x * 3x = 15x^2$.

Outer: $5x * 3 = 15x$.

Inner: $2 * 3x = 6x$.

Last: $2 * 3 = 6$.

Combine like terms: $15x^2 + 21x + 6$.

Example: Binomial * Polynomial.

$(x + 3)(2x^2 - 5x - 2)$.

First term: $x(2x^2 - 5x - 2) = 2x^3 - 5x^2 - 2x$.

Second term: $3(2x^2 - 5x - 2) = 6x^2 - 15x - 6$.

Added Together: $2x^3 + x^2 - 17x - 6$.

Distributive Property

When a variable is placed outside of a parenthetical set, it is *distributed* to all of the variables within that set.

$5(2y - 3x) = 10y - 15x$ [Can also be written as $(2y - 3x)5$].

$2x(3y + 1) + 6x = 6xy + 2x + 6x = 6xy + 8x$.

Combining Like Terms

This is exactly how it sounds! When a variable (x, y, z, r – anything!) is present in an equation, you can combine those terms with like variables.

$9r + 2r = 11r$.

$4x + 2y + 3 - 2x = 2x + 2y + 3$.

Arithmetic Sequence

Each term is equal to the previous term plus x.

Example: 2, 5, 8, 11.

$2 + 3 = 5$; $5 + 3 = 8$... etc.

$x = 3$.

Linear Systems

There are two different methods can be used to solve multiple equation linear systems:

Substitution Method: This solves for one variable in one equation and substitutes it into the other equation. **Example**: Solve: $3y - 4 + x = 0$ and $5x + 6y = 11$.

1. Step 1: Solve for one variable:
   $3y - 4 = 0$.
   $3y + x = 4$.
   $x = 4 - 3y$.

2. Step 2: Substitute into the second equation and solve:
   $5(4 - 3y) + 6y = 11$.
   $20 - 15y + 6y = 11$.
   $20 - 9y = 11$.
   $-9y = -9$.
   $y = 1$.

3. Step 3: Substitute into the first equation:
   $3(1) - 4 + x = 0$.
   $-1 + x = 0$.
   $x = 1$.

   Solution: $x = 1, y = 1$.

Addition Method: Manipulate one of the equations so that when it is added to the other, one variable is eliminated. **Example**: Solve: $2x + 4y = 8$ and $4x + 2y = 10$.

1. Step 1: Manipulate one equation to eliminate a variable when added together:
$-2(2x + 4y = 8)$.
$-4x - 8y = -16$.
$(-4x - 8y = -16) + (4x + 2y = 10)$.
$-6y = -6$.
$y = 1$.

2. Step 2: Plug into an equation to solve for the other variable:
$2x + 4(1) = 8$.
$2x + 4 = 8$.
$2x = 4$.
$x = 2$.

Solution: $x = 2$, $y = 1$.

Quadratics

Factoring: Converting $ax^2 + bx + c$ to factored form. Find two numbers that are factors of c and whose sum is b. **Example**: Factor: $2x^2 + 12x + 18 = 0$.

1. Step 1: If possible, factor out a common monomial: $2(x^2 - 6x + 9)$.

2. Step 2: Find two numbers that are factors of 9 and which equal -6 when added:
$2(x \quad)(x \quad)$.
$\quad -3 \quad , -3$

3. Step 3: Fill in the binomials. Be sure to check your answer signs.
$2(x - 3)(x - 3)$.

4. Step 4: To solve, set each to equal 0.
$x - 3 = 0$. So, $x = 3$.

Difference of squares:

$a^2 - b^2 = (a + b)(a - b)$.

$a^2 + 2ab + b^2 = (a + b)(a + b)$.

$a^2 - 2ab + b^2 = (a - b)(a - b)$.

Geometry

- **Acute Angle**: Measures less than 90°.

- **Acute Triangle**: Each angle measures less than 90°.

- **Obtuse Angle**: Measures greater than 90°.

- **Obtuse Triangle**: One angle measures greater than 90°.

- **Adjacent Angles**: Share a side and a vertex.

- **Complementary Angles**: Adjacent angles that sum to 90°.

- **Supplementary Angles**: Adjacent angles that sum to 180°.

- **Vertical Angles**: Angles that are opposite of each other. They are always congruent (equal in measure).

- **Equilateral Triangle**: All angles are equal.

- **Isosceles Triangle**: Two sides and two angles are equal.

- **Scalene**: No equal angles.

- **Parallel Lines**: Lines that will never intersect. Y ‖ X means line Y is parallel to line X.

- **Perpendicular lines**: Lines that intersect or cross to form 90° angles.

- **Transversal Line**: A line that crosses parallel lines.

- **Bisector**: Any line that cuts a line segment, angle, or polygon exactly in half.

- **Polygon**: Any enclosed plane shape with three or more connecting sides (ex. a triangle).

- **Regular Polygon**: Has all equal sides and equal angles (ex. square).

- **Arc**: A portion of a circle's edge.

- **Chord**: A line segment that connects two different points on a circle.

- **Tangent**: Something that touches a circle at only one point without crossing through it.

- **Sum of Angles**: The sum of angles of a polygon can be calculated using $(n-1)180^o$, when n = the number of sides.

Regular Polygons

Polygon Angle Principle
: S = The sum of interior angles of a polygon with n-sides.

$S = (n - 2)180.$

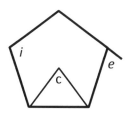

The measure of each central angle (c) is $360°/n$.
The measure of each interior angle (i) is $(n - 2)180°/n$.
The measure of each exterior angle (e) is $360°/n$.

To compare areas of similar polygons: $A_1/A_2 = (side_1/side_2)^2$.

Triangles

The angles in a triangle add up to $180°$.

Area of a triangle = $\frac{1}{2} * b * h$, or $\frac{1}{2}bh$.

Pythagoras' Theorem: $a^2 + b^2 = c^2$.

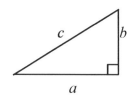

Trapezoids

Four-sided polygon, in which the bases (and only the bases) are parallel.
Isosceles Trapezoid – base angles are congruent.

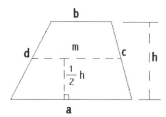

Area and Perimeter of a Trapezoid

$$m = \frac{1}{2}(a + b)$$

$$Area = \frac{1}{2}h * (a + b) = m * h$$

$$Perimeter = a + b + c + d = 2m + c + d$$

If m is the median then: m ll $\overline{AB}$ and m ll CD

Rhombus

Four-sided polygon, in which all four sides are congruent and opposite sides are parallel.

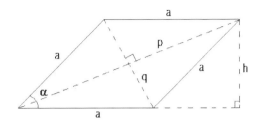

Area and Perimeter of a Rhombus

$$Perimeter = 4a$$

$$Area = a^2 \sin \alpha = a * h = \frac{1}{2}pq$$

$$4a^2 = p^2 + q^2$$

Rectangle

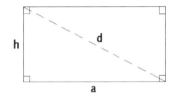

Area and Perimeter of a Rectangle

$$d = \sqrt{a^2 + h^2}$$

$$a = \sqrt{d^2 - h^2}$$

$$h = \sqrt{d^2 - a^2}$$

$$Perimeter = 2a + 2h$$

$$Area = a \cdot h$$

Square

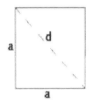

Area and Perimeter of a Square

$$d = a\sqrt{2}$$

$$Perimeter = 4a = 2d\sqrt{2}$$

$$Area = a^2 = \frac{1}{2}d^2$$

Circle

Area and Perimeter of a Circle

$$d = 2r$$

$$Perimeter = 2\pi r = \pi d$$

$$Area = \pi r^2$$

Cube

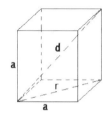

Area and Volume of a Cube

$$r = a\sqrt{2}$$

$$d = a\sqrt{3}$$

$$Area = 6a^2$$

$$Volume = a^3$$

Cuboid

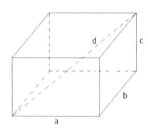

Area and Volume of a Cuboid

$$d = \sqrt{a^2 + b^2 + c^2}$$

$$A = 2(ab + ac + bc)$$

$$V = abc$$

Cylinder

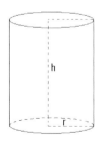

Area and Volume of a Cylinder

$$d = 2r$$

$$A_{surface} = 2\pi rh$$

$$A_{base} = 2\pi r^2$$

$$Area = A_{surface} + A_{base}$$

$$= 2\pi r\,(h + r)$$

$$Volume = \pi r^2 h$$

Mathematics Practice Test

ORDER OF OPERATIONS

1. $3 * (2 * 4^3) \div 4 =$ _____

2. $(4^3 + 2 - 1) =$ _____

3. $(5 * 3) * 1 + 5 =$ _____

4. $(7^2 - 2^3 - 6) =$ _____

5. $(5^3 + 7) * 2 =$ _____

ALGEBRA

6. **If Lynn can type a page in p minutes, how many pages can she do in 5 minutes?**

   a) $5/p$.
   b) $p - 5$.
   c) $p + 5$.
   d) $p/5$.
   e) $1 - p + 5$.

7. **If Sally can paint a house in 4 hours, and John can paint the same house in 6 hours, then how long will it take for both of them to paint the house together?**

   a) 2 hours and 24 minutes.
   b) 3 hours and 12 minutes.
   c) 3 hours and 44 minutes.
   d) 4 hours and 10 minutes.
   e) 4 hours and 33 minutes.

8. **The sales price of a car is $12,590, which is 20% off the original price. What is the original price?**

   a) $14,310.40.
   b) $14,990.90.
   c) $15,290.70.
   d) $15,737.50.
   e) $16,935.80.

9. Solve the following equation for a: $2a \div 3 = 8 + 4a$.

    a) -2.4.
    b) 2.4.
    c) 1.3.
    d) -1.3.
    e) 0.

10. If $y = 3$, then what is $y^3(y^3 - y)$?

    a) 300.
    b) 459.
    c) 648.
    d) 999.
    e) 1099.

ALGEBRA 2

11. The average of three numbers is v. If one of the numbers is z and another is y, then what is the remaining number?

    a) $ZY - V$.
    b) $Z/V - 3 - Y$.
    c) $Z/3 - V - Y$.
    d) $3V - Z - Y$.
    e) $V - Z - Y$.

12. Mary is reviewing her algebra quiz. She has determined that one of her solutions is incorrect. Which one is it?

    a) $2x + 5(x - 1) = 9; x = 2$.
    b) $p - 3(p - 5) = 10; p = 2.5$.
    c) $4y + 3y = 28; y = 4$.
    d) $5w + 6w - 3w = 64; w = 8$.
    e) $t - 2t - 3t = 32; t = 8$.

13. What simple interest rate will Susan need to secure in order to make $2,500 in interest on a $10,000 principal over 5 years?

    a) 4%.
    b) 5%.
    c) 6%.
    d) 7%.
    e) 8%.

14. Which of the following is not a rational number?

    a) – 4.
    b) 1/5.
    c) 0.8333333...
    d) 0.45.
    e) $\sqrt{2}$.

AVERAGES and ROUNDING

15. Round 907.457 to the nearest tens place.

    a) 908.0.
    b) 910.
    c) 907.5.
    d) 900.
    e) 907.46.

16. What is 1230.932567 rounded to the nearest hundredths place?

    a) 1200.
    b) 1230.9326.
    c) 1230.93.
    d) 1230.
    e) 1230.933.

17. Subtract the following numbers and round to the nearest tenths place:
        134.679
       – 45.548
       – 67.8807

    a) 21.3.
    b) 21.25.
    c) -58.97.
    d) -59.0.
    e) 1.

18. What is the absolute value of –9?

    a) –9.
    b) 9.
    c) 0.
    d) –1.
    e) 1.

19. What is the median of the following list of numbers: 4, 5, 7, 9, 10, and 12?

   a) 6.
   b) 7.5.
   c) 7.8.
   d) 8.
   e) 9.

20. What is the mathematical average of the number of weeks in a year, seasons in a year, and the number of days in January?

   a) 36.
   b) 33.
   c) 32.
   d) 31.
   e) 29.

BASIC OPERATIONS
21. Add 0.98 + 45.102 + 32.3333 + 31 + 0.00009.

   a) 368.573.
   b) 210.536299.
   c) 109.41539.
   d) 99.9975.
   e) 80.8769543.

22. Find 0.12 ÷ 1.

   a) 12.
   b) 1.2.
   c) .12.
   d) .012.
   e) .0012.

23. (9 ÷ 3) * (8 ÷ 4) equals:

   a) 1.
   b) 6.
   c) 72.
   d) 576.
   e) 752.

24. 6 * 0 * 5 equals:

    a) 30.
    b) 11.
    c) 25.
    d) 0.
    e) 27.

25. 7.95 ÷ 1.5 equals:

    a) 2.4.
    b) 5.3.
    c) 6.2.
    d) 7.3.
    e) 7.5.

ESTIMATION SEQUENCE

26. Describe the following sequence in mathematical terms: 144, 72, 36, 18, and 9.

    a) Descending arithmetic sequence.
    b) Ascending arithmetic sequence.
    c) Descending geometric sequence.
    d) Ascending geometric sequence.
    e) Miscellaneous sequence.

27. Which of the following is not a whole number followed by its square?

    a) 1, 1.
    b) 6, 36.
    c) 8, 64.
    d) 10, 100.
    e) 11, 144.

28. There are 12 more apples than oranges in a basket of 36 apples and oranges. How many apples are in the basket?

    a) 12.
    b) 15.
    c) 24.
    d) 28.
    e) 36.

29. Which of the following correctly identifies 4 consecutive odd integers, where the sum of the middle two integers is equal to 24?

    a) 5, 7, 9, 11.
    b) 7, 9, 11, 13.
    c) 9, 11, 13, 15.
    d) 11, 13, 15, 17.
    e) 13, 15, 17, 19.

30. What is the next number in the sequence? 6, 12, 24, 48, ___ .

    a) 72.
    b) 96.
    c) 108.
    d) 112.
    e) 124.

MEASUREMENT PRACTICE

31. If a rectangular house has a perimeter of 44 yards, and a length of 36 feet, what is the house's width?

    a) 30 feet.
    b) 18 yards.
    c) 28 feet.
    d) 32 feet.
    e) 36 yards.

32. What is the volume of a cylinder with a diameter of 1 foot and a height of 14 inches?

    a) 2104.91cubic inches.
    b) 1584 cubic inches.
    c) 528 cubic inches.
    d) 904.32 cubic inches.
    e) 264 cubic inches.

33. What is the volume of a cube whose width is 5 inches?

    a) 15 cubic inches.
    b) 25 cubic inches.
    c) 64 cubic inches.
    d) 100 cubic inches.
    e) 125 cubic inches.

34. A can's diameter is 3 inches, and its height is 8 inches. What is the volume of the can?

    a) 50.30 cubic inches.
    b) 56.57 cubic inches.
    c) 75.68 cubic inches.
    d) 113.04 cubic inches.
    e) 226.08 cubic inches.

35. If the area of a square flowerbed is 16 square feet, then how many feet is the flowerbed's perimeter?

    a) 4.
    b) 12.
    c) 16.
    d) 20.
    e) 24.

PERCENT and RATIO

36. If a discount of 25% off the retail price of a desk saves Mark $45, what was desk's original price?

    a) $135.
    b) $160.
    c) $180.
    d) $210.
    e) $215.

37. A customer pays $1,100 in state taxes on a newly-purchased car. What is the value of the car if state taxes are 8.9% of the value?

    a) $9.765.45.
    b) $10,876.90.
    c) $12,359.55.
    d) $14,345.48.
    e) $15,745.45.

38. How many years does Steven need to invest his $3,000 at 7% to earn $210 in simple interest?

    a) 1 year.
    b) 2 years.
    c) 3 years.
    d) 4 years.
    e) 5 years.

39. 35% of what number is 70?

a) 100.
b) 110.
c) 150.
d) 175.
e) 200.

40. What number is 5% of 2000?

a) 50.
b) 100.
c) 150.
d) 200.
e) 250.

COMBINED MATHEMATIC CONCEPTS PRACTICE

41. How long will Lucy have to wait before for her $2,500 invested at 6% earns $600 in simple interest?

a) 2 years.
b) 3 years.
c) 4 years.
d) 5 years.
e) 6 years.

42. If $r = 5z$ and $15z = 3y$, then r equals:

a) y.
b) $2y$.
c) $5y$.
d) $10y$.
e) $15y$.

43. What is 35% of a number if 12 is 15% of that number?

a) 5.
b) 12.
c) 28.
d) 33.
e) 62.

44. A computer is on sale for $1,600, which is a 20% discount off the regular price. The regular price is?

   a) $1800.
   b) $1900.
   c) $2000.
   d) $2100.
   e) $2200.

45. A car dealer sells an SUV for $39,000, which represents a 25% profit over the cost. What was the cost of the SUV to the dealer?

   a) $29,250.
   b) $31,200.
   c) $32,500.
   d) $33,800.
   e) $33,999.

46. Employees of a discount appliance store receive an additional 20% off of the lowest price on an item. If an employee purchases a dishwasher during a 15% off sale, how much will he pay if the dishwasher originally cost $450?

   a) $280.90.
   b) $287.
   c) $292.50.
   d) $306.
   e) $333.89.

47. The city council has decided to add a 0.3% tax on motel and hotel rooms. If a traveler spends the night in a motel room that costs $55 before taxes, how much will the city receive in taxes from him?

   a) 10 cents.
   b) 11 cents.
   c) 15 cents.
   d) 17 cents.
   e) 21 cents.

48. Grace has 16 jellybeans in her pocket. She has 8 red ones, 4 green ones, and 4 blue ones. What is the minimum number of jellybeans she must take out of her pocket to ensure that she has one of each color?
   a) 4.
   b) 8.
   c) 12.
   d) 13.
   e) 16.

49. You need to purchase a textbook for nursing school. The book costs $80.00, and the sales tax is 8.25%. You have $100. How much change will you receive back?

   a) $5.20.
   b) $7.35.
   c) $13.40.
   d) $19.95.
   e) $21.25.

50. Your supervisor instructs you to purchase 240 pens and 6 staplers for the nurse's station. Pens are purchased in sets of 6 for $2.35 per pack. Staplers are sold in sets of 2 for $12.95. How much will purchasing these products cost?

   a) $132.85.
   b) $145.75.
   c) $162.90.
   d) $225.25.
   e) $226.75.

51. Two cyclists start biking from a trailhead at different speeds and times. The second cyclist travels at 10 miles per hour and starts 3 hours after the first cyclist, who is traveling at 6 miles per hour. Once the second cyclist starts biking, how much time will pass before he catches up with the first cyclist?

   a) 2 hours.
   b) 4 ½ hours.
   c) 5 ¾ hours.
   d) 6 hours.
   e) 7 ½ hours.

52. Jim can fill a pool with water by the bucket-full in 30 minutes. Sue can do the same job in 45 minutes. Tony can do the same job in 1 ½ hours. How quickly can all three fill the pool together?

   a) 12 minutes.
   b) 15 minutes.
   c) 21 minutes.
   d) 23 minutes.
   e) 28 minutes.

53. A study reported that, in a random sampling of 100 women over the age of 35, 8 of the women had been married 2 or more times. Based on the study results, how many women over the age of 35 in a group of 5,000 would likely have been married 2 or more times?

   a) 55.
   b) 150.
   c) 200.
   d) 400.
   e) 600.

54. John is traveling to a meeting that is 28 miles away. He needs to be there in 30 minutes. How fast does he need to go in order to make it to the meeting on time?

   a) 25 mph.
   b) 37 mph.
   c) 41 mph.
   d) 49 mph.
   e) 56 mph.

55. If Steven can mix 20 drinks in 5 minutes, Sue can mix 20 drinks in 10 minutes, and Jack can mix 20 drinks in 15 minutes, then how much time will it take all 3 of them working together to mix the 20 drinks?

   a) 2 minutes and 44 seconds.
   b) 2 minutes and 58 seconds.
   c) 3 minutes and 10 seconds.
   d) 3 minutes and 26 seconds.
   e) 4 minutes and 15 seconds.

56. Jim's belt broke, and his pants are falling down. He has 5 pieces of string. He needs to choose the piece that will be able to go around his 36-inch waist. The piece must be at least 4 inches longer than his waist so that he can tie a knot in it, but it cannot be more that 6 inches longer so that the ends will not show from under his shirt. Which of the following pieces of string will work the best?

   a) 3 feet.
   b) 3 ¾ feet.
   c) 3 5/8 feet.
   d) 3 1/3 feet.
   e) 2 ½ feet.

57. In the final week of January, a car dealership sold 12 cars. A new sales promotion came out the first week of February, and the dealership sold 19 cars that week. What was the percent increase in sales from the last week of January compared to the first week of February?

    a) 58%.
    b) 119%.
    c) 158%.
    d) 175%.
    e) 200%.

58. If two planes leave the same airport at 1:00 PM, how many miles apart will they be at 3:00 PM if one travels directly north at 150 mph and the other travels directly west at 200 mph?

    a) 50 miles.
    b) 100 miles.
    c) 500 miles.
    d) 700 miles.
    e) 1,000 miles.

59. During a 5-day festival, the number of visitors tripled each day. If the festival opened on a Thursday with 345 visitors, what was the attendance on that Sunday?

    a) 345.
    b) 1,035.
    c) 1,725.
    d) 3,105.
    e) 9,315.

60. What will it cost to carpet a room with indoor/outdoor carpet if the room is 10 feet wide and 12 feet long? The carpet costs $12.51 per square yard.

    a) $166.80.
    b) $175.90.
    c) $184.30.
    d) $189.90.
    e) $192.20.

61. Sally has three pieces of material. The first piece is 1 yard, 2 feet, and 6 inches long; the second piece is 2 yard, 1 foot, and 5 inches long; and the third piece is 4 yards, 2 feet, and 8 inches long. How much material does Sally have?
    a) 7 yards, 1 foot, and 8 inches.
    b) 8 yards, 4 feet, and 4 inches.
    c) 8 yards and 11 inches.
    d) 9 yards and 7 inches.
    e) 10 yards.

62. A vitamin's expiration date has passed. It was supposed to contain 500 mg of Calcium, but it has lost 325 mg of Calcium. How many mg of Calcium are left?
    a) 135 mg.
    b) 175 mg.
    c) 185 mg.
    d) 200 mg.
    e) 220 mg.

63. You have orders to give a patient 20 mg of a certain medication. The medication is stored as 4 mg per 5-mL dose. How many milliliters will need to be given?
    a) 15 mL.
    b) 20 mL.
    c) 25 mL.
    d) 30 mL.
    e) 35 mL.

64. You need a 1680 ft^3 aquarium, exactly, for your fish. The pet store has four choices of aquariums. The length, width, and height are listed on the box, but not the volume. Which of the following aquariums would fit your needs?
    a) 12 ft by 12 ft by 12 ft.
    b) 13 ft by 15 ft by 16 ft.
    c) 14 ft by 20 ft by 6 ft.
    d) 15 ft by 16 ft by 12 ft.
    e) 15 ft by 12 ft by 12 ft.

65. Sabrina's boss states that she will increase Sabrina's salary from $12,000 to $14,000 per year if Sabrina enrolls in business courses at a local community college. What percent increase in salary will result from Sabrina taking the business courses?
    a) 15%.
    b) 16.7%.
    c) 17.2%.
    d) 85%.
    e) 117%.

66. Jim works for $15.50 per hour at a health care facility. He is supposed to get a $0.75 per hour raise after one year of service. What will be his percent increase in hourly pay?

   a) 2.7%.
   b) 3.3%.
   c) 133%.
   d) 4.8%.
   e) 105%.

67. Edmond has to sell his BMW. He bought the car for $49,000, but sold it at 20% less. At what price did Edmond sell the car?

   a) $24,200.
   b) $28,900.
   c) $35,600.
   d) $37,300.
   e) $39,200.

68. At a company fish fry, half of those in attendance are employees. Employees' spouses make up a third of the attendance. What is the percentage of the people in attendance who are neither employees nor employees' spouses?

   a) 10.5%.
   b) 16.7%.
   c) 25%.
   d) 32.3%.
   e) 38%.

69. If Sam can do a job in 4 days that Lisa can do in 6 days and Tom can do in 2 days, how long would the job take if Sam, Lisa, and Tom worked together to complete it?

   a) 0.8 days.
   b) 1.09 days.
   c) 1.23 days.
   d) 1.65 days.
   e) 1.97 days.

70. Sarah needs to make a cake and some cookies. The cake requires 3/8 cup of sugar, and the cookies require 3/5 cup of sugar. Sarah has 15/16 cups of sugar. Does she have enough sugar, or how much more does she need?

    a) She has enough sugar.
    b) She needs 1/8 of a cup of sugar.
    c) She needs 3/80 of a cup of sugar.
    d) She needs 4/19 of a cup of sugar.
    e) She needs 1/9 of a cup of sugar.

GEOMETRY

71. What is the area outside the circle, but within the square whose two corners are A and B?

A(3,5)   B (8,17)

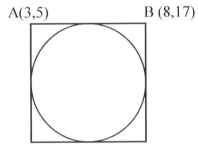

    a) 169(1- π)
    b) 169 π
    c) 169 π /4
    d) 169(1- π /4)
    e) 169

72. What is the area, in square feet, of the triangle whose sides have lengths equal to 3, 4, and 5 feet?

    a) 6 square feet
    b) 7 square feet
    c) 4 square feet
    d) 5 square feet
    e) 8 square feet

73. In the following figure, where AE bisects line BC, and angles AEC and AEB are both right angles, what is the length of AB?

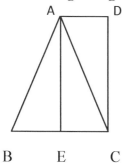

BC = 6 cm
AD = 3 cm
CD = 4 cm

   a) 1 cm
   b) 2 cm
   c) 3 cm
   d) 4 cm
   e) 5 cm

74. In the following triangle, if AB = 6 and BC = 8, what should the length of CA be to make triangle ABC a right triangle?

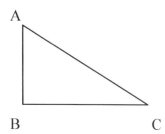

   a) 10
   b) 9
   c) 8
   d) 4
   e) 7

75. In the following circle there is a square with an area of 36 cm^2. What is the area outside the square, but within the circle?

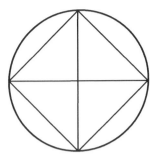

    a) 18 π cm^2
    b) 18 π - 30 cm^2
    c) 18 π - 36 cm^2
    d) 18 cm^2
    e) -18 cm^2

76. If a square of area 25 cm^2 is rotated around the side AB, what is the volume of the resulting shape?

    a) 625
    b) 625 π
    c) 125 π
    d) 25 π^2
    e) 625 π^2

77. The length of a rectangle is 4 times its width. If the width of the rectangle is 5 - x inches and the perimeter of the rectangle is 30 inches, what is x?

    a) 1
    b) 2
    c) 3
    d) 4
    e) 5

78. If in triangle ABC, AB:AC = 6:10, then what is BC/AC?

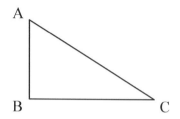

    a) 8:10
    b) 6:8
    c) 4:5
    d) 2:5
    e) 5:8

79. If the diameter of a circle is doubled, the area increases by what factor?

    a) 1 time
    b) 2 times
    c) 3 times
    d) 4 times
    e) 5 times

80. A rectangular prism's length = 4 cm, width = 5 cm, and height = 10 cm. It weighs 6 kg. If the length is cut in half, the width is doubled, and the height stays the same, how much will the resulting rectangular prism weigh?

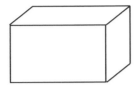

    a) 6 kg
    b) 3 kg
    c) 200 g
    d) 400 g
    e) 5 kg

81. In the following figure, what is A?

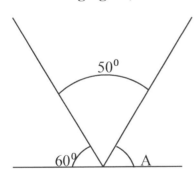

    a) 110^0
    b) 70^0
    c) 180^0
    d) 50^0
    e) 55^0

82. In the following isosceles triangle, what is the largest possible value of angle B?

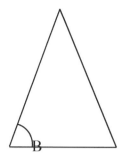

a) 59.5^0
b) 45.0^0
c) 90.0^0
d) 89.5^0
e) 30.5^0

83. In the following figure, what are the values of angles A, B and C?

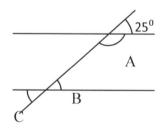

a) $\angle A = 155^0, \angle B = 25^0, \angle C = 25^0$
b) $\angle A = 145^0, \angle B = 20^0, \angle C = 20^0$
c) $\angle A = 150^0, \angle B = 25^0, \angle C = 25^0$
d) $\angle A = 55^0, \angle B = 35^0, \angle C = 45^0$
e) $\angle A = 155^0, \angle B = 35^0, \angle C = 25^0$

84. In the following triangle PQR, what is the measure of angle A?

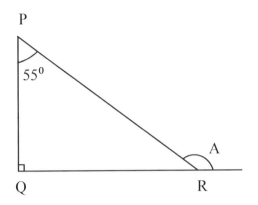

a) 145^0
b) 140^0
c) 70^0
d) 50^0
e) 40^0

EXPONENTS & ROOTS

85. What is $x^2y^3z^5/y^2z^{-9}$?

a) y^5z^4
b) yz^4
c) x^2yz^{14}
d) $x^2y^5z^4$
e) xyz

86. What is k if $(2m^3)^5 = 32m^{k+1}$?

a) 11
b) 12
c) 13
d) 14
e) 15

87. What is $x^5y^4z^3/x^{-3}y^2z^{-4}$?

a) $x^6y^4z^7$
b) x^8yz^7
c) x^6yz^7
d) $x^8y^2z^7$
e) $x^6y^2z^7$

88. Evaluate $(a^2 * a^{54} + a^{56} + (a^{58}/a^2))/a^4$.

    a) a^{56}
    b) $3a^{56}$
    c) $3a^{52}$
    d) $3a^{54}$
    e) a^{54}

89. $9^m = 3^{-1/n}$. What is mn?

    a) .5
    b) 2
    c) -2
    d) -.5
    e) -1

90. If $2^a * 4^a = 32$, what is a?

    a) 1/3
    b) 2/3
    c) 1
    d) 4/3
    e) 5/3

91. Evaluate $\sqrt{3} + 2\sqrt{3} * \sqrt{3} + (\sqrt{3})^2 + \sqrt[4]{256}$

    a) 16
    b) 13
    c) $\sqrt{3} + \sqrt{13}$
    d) 4
    e) $13 + \sqrt{3}$

92. The number 568cd should be divisible by 2, 5, and 7. What are the values of the digits c and d?

    a) 56835
    b) 56830
    c) 56860
    d) 56840
    e) 56800

93. What is the value of f(x) = (x²-25)/(x+5) when x = 0?

    a) -1
    b) -2
    c) -3
    d) -4
    e) -5

94. If x = 5y + 4, what is the value of y if x = 29?

    a) 33/5
    b) 5.5
    c) 5
    d) 0
    e) 29/5

95. Expand (3x - 4)(6 - 2x).

    a) $6x^2 - 6x + 8$
    b) $-6x^2 + 26x - 24$
    c) $6x^2 - 26x + 24$
    d) $-6x^2 + 26x + 24$
    e) $6x^2 + 26x - 24$

96. If 6n + m is divisible by 3 and 5, which of the following numbers when added to 6n + m will still give a result that is divisible by 3 and 5?

    a) 4
    b) 6
    c) 12
    d) 20
    e) 60

97. If x is negative, and x³/5 and x/5 both give the same result, what could be the value of x?

    a) -5
    b) -4
    c) 3
    d) 0
    e) -1

98. Simplify: $30(\sqrt{40} - \sqrt{60})$.

    a) $30(\sqrt{5} - \sqrt{15})$
    b) $30(\sqrt{10} + \sqrt{15})$
    c) $60(\sqrt{5} + \sqrt{15})$
    d) $60(\sqrt{10} - \sqrt{15})$
    e) 60

99. Simplify: $30/(\sqrt{40} - \sqrt{60})$.

    a) $3(\sqrt{5} + \sqrt{15})$
    b) $-3(\sqrt{5} - \sqrt{15})$
    c) $-3(\sqrt{10} + \sqrt{15})$
    d) $3(\sqrt{10} + \sqrt{15})$
    e) $3(\sqrt{10} - \sqrt{15})$

100. What is the least common multiple of 2, 3, 4, and 5?

    a) 30
    b) 60
    c) 120
    d) 40
    e) 50

MATH ANSWER KEY

1. 96	26.c)	51.b)	76. c)
2. 65	27.e)	52.b)	77. b)
3. 20	28.c)	53.d)	78. a)
4. 35	29.c)	54.e)	79. d)
5. 264	30.b)	55.a)	80. a)
6. a)	31.a)	56.d)	81. b)
7. a)	32.b)	57.a)	82. d)
8. d)	33.e)	58.c)	83. a)
9. a)	34.b)	59.e)	84. a)
10.c)	35.c)	60.a)	85. c)
11.d)	36.c)	61.d)	86. d)
12.e)	37.c)	62.b)	87. d)
13.b)	38.a)	63.c)	88. c)
14.e)	39.e)	64.c)	89. d)
15.b)	40.b)	65.b)	90. e)
16.c)	41.c)	66.d)	91. e)
17.a)	42.a)	67.e)	92. d)
18.b)	43.c)	68.b)	93. e)
19.d)	44.c)	69.b)	94. c)
20.e)	45.b)	70. c)	95. b)
21.c)	46.d)	71. d)	96. e)
22.c)	47.d)	72. a)	97. e)
23.b)	48.d)	73. e)	98. d)
24.d)	49.c)	74. a)	99. c)
25.b)	50.a)	75. c)	100.b)

Math Answer Explanations

1. Answer: 96

  Explanation: We need to remember the order of operations (PEMDAS) to solve this question. First of all, we solve the parenthesis, and then the exponents. In this particular question, 4^3 is within the parenthesis so we solve it first. $4^3 = 64$. Now, multiplying it with 2 to solve the parenthesis, it becomes $64*2 = 128$. So, the expression becomes $3*128 \div 4$. Following PEMDAS, we multiply 128 by 3, and then divide the answer by 4. This gives us $384 \div 4 = 96$

2. Answer: 65

  Explanation: We need to remember the order of operations (PEMDAS) to solve this question. First of all, we solve the parenthesis, and then the exponents. In this particular question, 4^3 is within the parenthesis so we solve it first. $4^3 = 64$. Now, the expression becomes (64+2-1). So, we add 2 in 64 first, and then subtract 1 from the answer. This gives us 66-1 = 5.

3. Answer: 20

  Explanation: This question also involves the order of operations (PEMDAS). To solve this question, we solve the parenthesis first, and then multiply the answer by 1. After that, we add 5 to get our final answer. (5*3) = 15, so the expression becomes 15*1+5 = 15 + 5 = 20

4. Answer: 35

  Explanation: We need to remember the order of operations (PEMDAS) to solve this question. First of all, we solve the parenthesis, and then the exponents. However, in order to solve the parenthesis, we need to know the values of 7^2 and 2^3. Therefore, we find these exponents first and then proceed with PEMDAS. Since $7^2 = 49$ and $2^3 = 8$, the expression becomes (49-8-6) i.e. we simply subtract 6 and 8 from 49 to get our final answer which is equal to 35.

5. Answer: 264

  Explanation: First of all, we find the value of 5^3 to solve the parenthesis (remember the order of operations PEMDAS). As we know that $5^3 = 5*5*5 = 125$, the expression becomes (125+7)*2.
  We solve the parenthesis first because it is given more preference in PEMDAS, it becomes132*2.
  Multiplying these two numbers, we get our final answer which is 264.

6. Answer: Option(a)

  Explanation: From the given information in the question, Lynn writes one page in 'p' minutes. Now, we are asked about the number of pages Lynn can write in 5 minutes. The simplest way to solve this question is by writing it in ratio form I.e.
  1 page ➜ 'p' minutes
  X pages ➜ 5 minutes
  Cross multiplying the above equations, we get 5*1 =x*p
  Therefore, x = 5/p (Which means that he can type 5/p pages in 5 minutes)

7. Answer: Option (a)

   Explanation: Sally can paint a house in 4 hours means that in one hour, Sally paints ¼ of the house. Similarly, John can paint a house in 6 hours, which means that he paints $\frac{1}{6}$ of the house in 1 hour. If both Sally and John work together for one hour, they can paint (1/4 + 1/6) = 5/12 of the house. In order to paint the house completely, they would need 12/5 hours. Please note that 12/5 = 2.4 hours.

   If we multiply 2.4 with 60, we can find out the exact number of minutes they are taking. 2.4 * 60 = 144 minutes. From the given answer options, only answer (a) correspond to 144 minutes (i.e. 2 hours and 24 minutes).

8. Answer: Option (d)

   Explanation: The sales price of the car is 20% off the original price (20% discount) which means that the given price of $12590 is 80% of the original price. Let's say that 'x' is the original price of the car, then

   (80/100)*x = 12590 (i.e. 80% of 'x' equals $12590)
   Solving the above equation, x = 12590*(100/80) ➜ $15,737 Option (d)

9. Answer: Option (a)

   Explanation: We re-write this equation as $\frac{2a}{3}$ = 8+4a. Now, we multiply by 3 on both sides. The equation becomes 2a = 24 + 12a ➜ -24 = 10a ➜ **a= -2.4** Option (a)

10. Answer: Option (c)

   Explanation: It's a relatively simple question. The value of 'y' is given as 3. We know that 3^3 = 27. So, the expression becomes 27 * (27-3) = 27*24 ➜ **648** Option (c)

11. Answer: Option (d)

   Explanation: Let's suppose that the unknown number is 'w'. So, the average of three numbers becomes,

   $$\frac{W+Z+Y}{3} = V$$

   Multiplying by '3' on both sides, we get
   w+z+y = 3v
   W= 3v-z-y
   So, the unknown number equals 3V- Z -Y

126

12. Answer: Option (e)

Explanation: In these types of questions, we have to check each answer option to find out the desired answer. In this particular question, we are looking for the option which gives INCORRECT answer. (It's very important that you read the statement of the question correctly)

Option(a) ➔ 2(2) + 5(2-1) = 4+ 5 =9 Which gives the correct answer.
Option (b)➔ 2.5- 3(2.5 -5) = 10 which gives the correct answer.
Option (c)➔ 4(4)+ 3(4) = 28 which gives the correct answer
Option (d) ➔ 5(8) + 6(8) -3(8) = 64 which gives the correct answer
Option (e) ➔ 8 – 2(8) – 3(8) = -32 ≠ 32. Option (e) gives us incorrect answer, therefore, we choose this option.

13. Answer: Option (b)

Explanation: The principal amount is given as \$10,000 and the total interest generated on this amount in 5 years is \$2500. If we suppose that 'x' is the percentage of interest per year, then the equation becomes,
5 * (x/100) * 10000 = 2500
Solving for 'x', we get x = 5%.

14. Answer: Option (e)

Explanation: A rational number is the one which can be written in form of a simple fraction. If we observe closely, only option (e) gives us a number which cannot be written in form of a fraction.

15. Answer: Option (b)

Explanation: We are asked to round off 907.457 to the nearest tens place. As the tens place in 907.457 is '7' which is greater than 5, we make is 910.

16. Answer: Option (c)

Explanation: We are asked to round off this given number to the nearest hundredth place. Considering the numbers on the right of the decimal, our answer comes out to be 1230.93

17. Answer: Option (a)

Explanation: When we subtract 45.548 and 67.8807 from 134.679, we get 21.2503. Now, applying the rounding off rules, 21.3 (Note that we were asked to round off upto the nearest tenth place only)

18. Answer: Option (b)

Explanation: We know that the absolute value of any negative number gives the positive of that same number i.e. Absolute value of -9 is +9.

19. Answer: Option (d)

Explanation: In order to find the median of any given list, first of all, we need to check if the numbers are arranged in an ascending order or not. In this case, these given numbers are already arranged in order. Secondly, we need to check if the total number of entries in the list is even or odd. Since the total number of entries in this list is 6, and 6 is an even number, the median of this list equals the average of two entries which are at the middle of this list. i.e. Median $= \frac{7+9}{2} = 8$.

20. Answer: Option (e)

Explanation: We know that the total number of weeks in a year is 52, the total number of seasons in a year is 4, and the total number of days in month of January is 31. Taking average of these 3 numbers, we get

$\frac{52+4+31}{3} = 29$

21. Answer: Option (c)

Explanation: There are two ways to solve this question. Either you can add all the given numbers and find the exact answer. This method is time consuming and is less efficient. The second method to solve this question is by adding only the numbers on the left of the decimal and then comparing your answer with the answer choices that you are given. We add 45, 32 and 31 to get

45+32+31 = 108. Now, we can easily interpret that our answer must be very close to 108 when we add the decimal points as well for each given number. In the answer choices, Only option (c) gives us a number which is closest to 108. (Note that this method of approximation saves time but it is not very accurate if all the answer choices are very close to each other.)

22. Answer: Option (c)

Explanation: Any number divided by '1' gives the same number as a result. Therefore, 0.12/1 = 0.12

23. Answer: Option (b)

Explanation: This is a very simple question. All you need to know is PEMDAS rule. First of all, we solve what is within the parenthesis, and then we multiply the answers of each parenthesis.
9 divided by 3 equals 3.
8 divided by 4 equals 2.
We multiply 3 and 2 to get our final answer: 3*2 = 6

24. Answer: Option (d)

Explanation: Anything multiplied by zero gives zero as answer. We are multiplying 0 by 5 and 6, so the answer is still 0.

25. Answer: Option (b)

Explanation: It is a simple division question. When we divide 7.95 by 1.5, we get 5.3 as answer. In order to re-confirm your answer, you can cross check by multiplying 5.3 by 1.5, and it would give 7.95.

26. Answer: Option (c)

Explanation: From the given sequence of numbers, we note that the numbers start from the highest and gradually decrease (144 > 72 > 36 18 > 9). Because of this decreasing order, we are sure that these numbers are in descending order. Also, we note that every next number in this sequence is obtained by dividing the previous number by 2. Therefore, it is Descending Geometric Sequence. (Some students might confuse it with geometric sequence with arithmetic sequence but please note that, for a sequence to be arithmetic, the difference between any two consecutive numbers in that sequence must be the same.)

27. Answer: Option (e)

Explanation: We know that $11^2 = 121$ ➜ $121 \neq 144$.

Option (e) is 11, 144. Since we are to choose the option in which a whole number is not followed by its square, and we know that $11^2 = 121$ instead of 144, we select option(e).

28. Answer: Option (c)

Explanation: Let's suppose that there are 'x' oranges in the basket. From the given statement of the question, the number of apples is 12 more than the number of oranges i.e. x+12. Also, its given that the total number of apples and oranges is 36. Writing this information in form of an equation, it becomes:

x+ x+12 = 36

2x= 36-12

x= 24/2

x= 12

Number of apples = x + 12 ➜ 12+12 = 24 Option (c)

29. Answer: Option (c)

Explanation: We need to take care of two things in order to answer this question. Firstly, the numbers should be consecutive odd numbers. All given options meet this criterion. Secondly, we need to look for the option in which the middle two numbers give us a sum of 24. Only option (c) has numbers such that the sum of middle two is 24 (i.e. 11 + 13 = 24).

30. Answer: Option (b)

Explanation: If we observe closely, we note that every next number in this sequence is obtained by multiplying the previous number by 2. i.e.

48 = 24*2

24= 12*2

12= 6*2

Therefore, in order to find the next number in the sequence, we multiply 48 by 2.

48*2 = 96

31. Answer: Option (a)

Explanation: Please note that it's a tricky question. The perimeter of the rectangular house is given as 44 yards, and the length of the house is given as 36 feet (units are different).

1 yard = 3 feet

44 yards = 132 feet

As we know that the perimeter of the rectangular house equals,

Perimeter = 2*(length) + 2*(width)

132 = 2(36) + 2* width

Width = (132-72)/2 = 30 feet

32. Answer: Option (b)

Explanation: We know that the volume of a cylinder is given by the formula V= $\pi r^2 h$

Important thing to note in this question is that the diameter of the cylinder in given instead of its radius. Also, its given in feet instead of inches. So, we first convert it into inches i.e. 1 foot = 12 inches diameter. So, the radius becomes 12/2 = 6 inches.

Now, putting in the values of radius and height in the formula, we get

V= $(3.14)(6)^2(14)$ = 1584cubic inches.

33. Answer: Option (e)

Explanation: We are given with the width of the cube. As we know that all sides of the cube are equal to each other, we say that the length and height of this cube is also 5.

So, the volume of this cube becomes;

Volume = Length * Width * Height = 5 * 5 * 5 = 125

34. Answer: Option (b)

Explanation: The diameter of the can is given as 3 inches. The radius, therefore, becomes 1.5 (i.e. half of the diameter). Height of the can is given as 8 inches.

Volume = $\pi r^2 h$

V = $(3.14)(1.5)^2(8)$ = 56.52 cubic inches

35. Answer: Option (c)

Explanation: The area of this square flower bed is given as 16. This means that when the length and width of this square flowerbed was multiplied, we got 16. Only 4*4 gives us 16. Therefore, we are left with only one option for the length of the each side of this square i.e. 4.

Now, we know that the length of each side of the square flowerbed is 16, Therefore, the perimeter becomes 4+4+4+4 = 16.

Important thing to note in this question is that the flowerbed is a 'square'. If it were a rectangular flowerbed, it could have a perimeter of 16 or 20.

36. Answer: Option (c)

Explanation: From the given information in the question, we know that 25% of the actual price of desk is $45. If we write this in form of an equation, it becomes;

(25/100) * x = $45 (25% of 'x' equals $45)

x= 45/0.25 ➜ $180   Therefore, the actual price of the desk equals to $180.

37. Answer: Option (c)

Explanation: Let's suppose that the actual value of the taxes is 'x'. 8.9% of this value equals $1100. Writing this in form of an equation, we get:

(8.9/100)* x = 1100

x=1100/ 0.089 ➔ $12359

38. Answer: Option (a)

Explanation: We know that:

Interest = Principal Amount * Rate * Time

Putting values in this formula, we get

210 = 3000 * 0.07 * Time

Time = 210/ (3000*0.07) ➔ 1

Therefore, time required = 1 year.

39. Answer: Option (e)

Explanation: Let's suppose that the unknown number is 'x'. So, 35% of 'x' is equal to 70. Writing this in form of an equation,

(35/100)* x = 70

x = 70/0.35

x= 200

40. Answer: Option (b)

Explanation: In order to find 5% of 2000, we need to multiply 2000 by (5/100) i.e.

2000*0.05 = 100

41. Answer: Option (c)

Explanation: We know that:

In this given question, principal amount is $2500, interest is $600, and rate is 0.06.

Interest = Principal Amount * Rate * Time

Putting values in this formula, we get

600 = 2500 * 0.06 * Time

Time = 600/ (2500*0.07) ➔ 4

Therefore, time required = **4 years**.

42. Answer: Option (a)

Explanation: We are given with two equations in this question. Firstly, it's given that r = 5z.

Secondly, its given that 15z = 3y, and we are asked about the value of 'r' in terms of 'y'. If we divide the second equation by '3', we get 5z = y, but from the first equation (i.e. r = 5z), we know that 5z = r.

So, we conclude that r = 5z = y ➔ r = y

43. Answer: Option(c)

Explanation: This is a tricky question. We need to find 35% of a number but this number is unknown. But we are given with that fact that 12 is 15% of that number. So, we first find out that 12 is 15% of what number? In order to find that out, we write the following equation:

0.15* x = 12

x= 12/0.15 ➔80

Now, we need to find 35% of 80. This can be easily found by multiplying 80 by (35/100) i.e.

80* 0.35 = 28

44. Answer: Option (c)

Explanation: From the statement of the question, it is clear that when we take 20% off the price of computer, it costs $1600. This means that $1600 equals 80% of the actual price of the computer. Writing this in form of an equation;

0.8 * x = $1600

x = 1600/0.8

x = $2000 where 'x' is the actual price of the computer.

45. Answer: Option (b)

Explanation: First of all, you should know that 25% profit on the actual price means that we have multiplied the original price by 1.25 i.e. (1+ 0.25). So, in order to find the actual price of SUV, we divide it by 1.25. This gives us $39000/1.25 ➔ $31200 which is the original price of the SUV.

46. Answer: Option (d)

Explanation: The original price of the dishwasher is given as $450. Since it is on a 15% sale, the price of dishwasher becomes 0.85* 450 = $382.5 [Please note that we have multiplied by 0.85 because this item is on 15% sale. 15% = 0.15. When an item is on 15% sale, it means that you have to pay for 100-15 ➔ 85% of the actual amount] (20% = 0.20) The person buying this dishwasher is an employee of this store, so he gets an additional 20% discount on this item, So, the final amount which he needs to pay becomes 0.8* 382.5 = $306 [Note that we have multiplied by 0.80 because it is on further 20% sale. When an item is on 20% sale, it means that you have to pay for 100% - 20% ➔ 80% of the actual amount]

47. Answer: Option (d)

Explanation: Hotel chares a tax of 0.3% i.e. 0.3/100 = 0.003. Multiplying it with $55 gives us the amount of tax amount which hotel has charged to this traveler.

$55* 0.003 = $0.165

Note that the given answer choices are in cents and our answer is in dollars. We convert our answer in to cents by multiplying it with 100. It becomes 16.5 cents. The nearest possible option 17 cents which is Option (c).

48. Answer: Option (d)

Explanation: The best way to answer this question is by considering all the answer choices one by one. We start with option (a) and see if it's correct. Grace has a total of 16 jellybeans, and she takes out 4. It is quite possible that she took all the green or all blue jellybeans, and missing out the red colored jellybeans; therefore, option (a) doesn't ensure us that she took out a jellybean of each color. Considering option (b) and (c), we see that even if Grace takes out 8 or 12 jellybeans, she still can't be sure if she has got all colors or not i.e. it is quite possible that she took out all 8 red ones, or may be all 8 red ones and 4 green ones, and still missing out on blue jellybeans.

Thus, in order to be completely sure that she has taken out jellybeans of every color, she must take out at least 13 or more jellybeans. Since we are asked about the minimum number, we choose option (d).

49. Answer: Option (c)

Explanation: This is a tricky question. We are given with the sales tax percentage and the actual amount of the book. First of all, we need to find out the amount we would be charged for this including sales tax, and then we need to subtract it from 100, to find out the change we will receive from them.

8.5% tax on $80 becomes 0.085*80 = $6.8

So, the total amount that we will be charged becomes 80+ 6.8 = $86.8

Subtracting it from $100 to find the change, we get 100 – 86.8 = $13.40

50. Answer: Option (a)

Explanation: From the given information in the question, we get to know that the pens are sold in packs of 6 at $2.35 per pack, and we need to buy $\frac{240}{6}$ = 40 packs. Therefore, the total amount required for 240 pens is 40*2.35 = $94.

Also, the staplers are sold in sets of 2 at $12.95 per set, and we need to buy $\frac{6}{2}$ = 3 sets of staplers. Therefore, the total amount for staplers equals 3*12.95 = $38.85

Total cost = $94 + $38.85 ➔ $132.85

51. Answer: Option (b)

Explanation: Let these two cyclists be A and B. Cyclist A is travelling at a speed of 6 miles per hour. Cyclist B is travelling at 10 miles per hour. Cyclist A started cycling 3 hours before cyclist B, so in these 3 hours, he had already travelled 6*3 = 18 miles. Now, lets check the distances covered by each cyclist for every hour.

After 1 Hour ➔	Cyclist A = 18+6 = 24 miles
	Cyclist B = 10 miles
After 2 Hours ➔	Cyclist A = 24+6 = 30 miles
	Cyclist B = 10+10 = 20 miles
After 3 Hours ➔	Cyclist A = 30+6 = 36 miles
	Cyclist B = 20+10 = 30 miles
After 4 Hours ➔	Cyclist A = 36+6 = 42 miles
	Cyclist B = 30+10 = 40 miles

After 4.5 Hours ➜   Cyclist A = 42+3 = 45 miles (We have added 3 here because we are considering distance covered by cyclist A in half hour i.e. 6/2)

Cyclist B = 40 + 5 = 45 miles (We have added 5 here because we are considering distance covered by cyclist B in half hour i.e. 10/2)

Therefore, after 4.5 hours, both cyclists would have covered the same distance.

52. Answer: Option (b)

Explanation: We need to calculate the individual work rates of each of the three given persons.

Jim can fill the pool in 30 minutes i.e. in one minute, he can fill $\frac{1}{30}$ of the pool.

Sue can fill the pool in 45 minutes i.e. in one minute, Sue can fill $\frac{1}{45}$ of the pool.

Tony can fill the pool in $1\frac{1}{2}$ hour [90 minutes], i.e. in one minute, he can fill $\frac{1}{90}$ of the pool.

So, if Jim, Sue and Tony work together for 1 minute, they can fill $\frac{1}{30} + \frac{1}{45} + \frac{1}{90} = \frac{1}{15}$ of the pool. Therefore, in order to fill the pool completely working together, they would need 15 minutes.

53. Answer: Option (d)

Explanation: In a given sample of 100 women aged over 35, 8 have been married at least twice. In order to find out the number of women at least married twice, in a sample of 5000 women, we write the following ratio:

Sample Space :	Aged Above 35
100-women :	8 married at least twice
5000-women :	'x' married at least twice

Cross multiplying, we get x*100 = 8*5000
x =40000/100 ➜ 400

54. Answer: Option (e)

Explanation: The total distance which needs to be covered is 28 miles. Total time which John has to reach there is 30 minutes i.e. 0.5 hour.

As we know that speed $= \frac{Distance}{Time} = \frac{28\ miles}{0.5\ hours} = 56$ miles/hour

55. Answer: Option (a)

Explanation: Steven can mix 20 drinks in 5 minutes, which means that in one minute, he can mix $\frac{20}{5}$ = 4 drinks.

Sue can mix 20 drinks in 10 minutes which means that Sue can mix $\frac{20}{10}$ = 2 drinks per minute.

Jack can mix 20 drinks in 15 minutes which means that he can mix $\frac{20}{15}$ = 1.33 drinks per minute.

Therefore, if Steven, Sue and Jack work together for one minute, they can mix 4+2+1.33 = 7.33 drinks per minutes. In order to mix a total of 20 drinks working together, they will need
$\frac{20}{7.33}$ = 2.72 minutes.

In order to find the exact seconds, we multiply our answer by 60. This gives us 60*2.72 = 163.7 seconds. We know that 163.7 correspond to 2 minutes and 44 seconds (approx).

56. Answer: Option (d)

Explanation: From the statement of the question, it is clear that we need string that is at least 40 inches long (i.e. 36 inch waist and 4 inches for knot) but not longer than 42 inches. Let's examine the length of strings available in answer options.

Option (a) = 3 feet = 36 inches Incorrect
Option (b) = 3(3/4) feet = 45 inches Incorrect
Option (c) = 3(5/8) feet = 43.5 inches Incorrect
Option (d) = 3 (1/3) feet = 40 inches **Correct**
Option (e) = 2(1/2) feet = 30 inches Incorrect

57. Answer: Option (a)

Explanation: In order to find the percentage change, we use the following formula.

Percentage Change = $\frac{Final\ value - Original\ Value}{Original\ Value}*100$

Therefore, percentage increase becomes, $\frac{19-12}{12}*100$ = 58%

58. Answer: Option (c)

Explanation: It's a tricky question. First of all, you must note that one plane is flying toward north, and the other one is flying towards west. The total distance between these two cannot be calculated by simply adding their individual distances. We need to use Pythagoras theorem to solve this question. Both airplanes left the airport at same time 1:00 pm and we looking for how much apart they would be after two hours at 3:00 pm.

Plane flying toward north has a speed of 150 miles per hour, so in two hours, it would have covered 300 miles.

Plane flying towards west has a speed of 200 miles per hours, so it would have covered 400 miles in two hours.

Using Pythagoras Theorem, We find the distance between these two planes as:

Distance = $\sqrt{(300)^2 + (400)^2}$ = 500 miles

59. Answer: Option (e)

Explanation: The number of people on Thursday is 345. Every next day the number of people triples. On Friday, it becomes 3*345 = 1035

On Saturday, the number of people who came to this festival became 3 * 1035 =3105

On Sunday, the number of people who came to this festival became 3 * 3105 = 9315

60. Answer: Option (a)

Explanation: It is important to note that the rate of the carpet is given is per sq. yard and the dimensions of the room are given in feet. So, we need to convert the width and length of the room in yards, and then calculate the total area of the room. We know that 1 foot = 0.33 yards

10 feet = 3.33 yards

12 feet = 4 yards

Area of the room = 4*3.33 = 13.32 sq yards

So, the total cost to carpet this room equals 13.32 * 12.51 ➜ $166.6

61. Answer: Option (d)

Explanation: First of all, we add the inches, feet and yards individually.

Inches: 6 + 5+ 8 = 19 inches

Feet = 2 + 1 + 2 = 5 Feet

Yards = 1 + 2 + 4 = 7 yards

As we know that there are 12 inches in 1 foot, so 19 inches becomes 1 foot and 7 inches. Therefore, we add one more to 5 feet, which makes it 6 feet.

Also, we know that 1 foot = 0.33 yards, so 6 feet = 2 yards.

This makes the total length equal to 9 yards and 7 inches. [9 yards because 7 yards calculated in the first step plus 2 yards from 6 feet conversion to yards.]

62. Answer: Option (b)

Explanation: The amount of calcium actually required was 500 mg in that vitamin, but it has lost 325mg of calcium in it. Therefore, it has got 500-325 = 175 mg calcium left in it after expiration.

63. Answer: Option (c)

Explanation: There are 4mg of medication in 5 mL dose. We need to give 20 mg to the patient and $\frac{20}{4} = 5$ so we multiply the dose by 5 to give our desired amount of medication to the patient. Therefore, 5* 5mL = 25 mL

64. Answer: Option (c)

Explanation: We know that the volume is given my formula length* width * height. In order to find the correct volume of the aquariums given in the answer options, we multiply their respective length, width and heights to see, which on equals to 1680.

Option (a) = 12*12*12 = 1728

Option (b) = 13*15*16 = 3120

Option (c) = 14*20*6 = 1680 which is our required answer. No need to check further options.

65. Answer: Option (b)

Explanation: If she takes the business courses, her salary would increase from $12000 to $14000. We know that

Percentage Change $= \frac{Final\ value - Original\ Value}{Original\ Value} * 100$ ➡ $\frac{14000-12000}{12000} * 100$

$\frac{2000}{12000} * 100 = 16.7\%$

66. Answer: Option (d)

Explanation: His new hourly salary would become $15.50+$0.75 = $16.25

Percentage change $= \frac{Final\ value - Original\ Value}{Original\ Value} * 100$

$\frac{16.25-15.50}{15.50} * 100$

$\frac{0.75}{15.50} * 100 = 4.8\%$

67. Answer: Option (e)

Explanation: Price of Edmond's car was $49000 but he had to sell it at 20% less. This means that the price at which he sold his car was 80% of the actual price. Therefore, 0.8*49000 = $39200

68. Answer: Option (b)

Explanation: The easiest way to solve these types of questions is to imagine a constant number. Let's say there are 100 people in the fish fry company, such that one half of the people are employee i.e. 100/2 = 50 employees.

Similarly, the spouses of the employees make one third of the attendance i.e. $\frac{100}{3} = 33.3$

Now, the remaining people are 100- 50 – 33.3 = 16.7 %

(Note: It is not possible that there are 33.3 or 16.7 person in the restraint. The number of people is always a whole number. But in this case while solving this question, we have used percentage approximation)

69. Answer: Option (b)

Explanation: First of all, we need to calculate the individual work rate for each of the given persons.

Sam can do that job in 4 days means that he can do ¼ of that job in a single day.

Lisa can do that same job in 6 days means that she can complete $\frac{1}{6}$ of the job in one day.

Tom can complete that job in 2 days, means that he can complete ½ of that job in one day.

So, if Sam, Lisa, and Tom work together for one day, they can complete $(\frac{1}{4} + \frac{1}{6} + \frac{1}{2}) =$ 0.917 job in a single day.

In order to complete 1 job working together, they would need 1/0.917 = 1.09 Days

70. Answer: Option (c)

Explanation: Cake requires $\frac{3}{8} = 0.375$ cup of sugar, whereas, cookies require $\frac{3}{5} = 0.6$ cup of sugar. This makes a total of $0.375 + 0.6 = 0.975$ cup of sugar.

Sarah has got $\frac{15}{16} = 0.9375$ cup of sugar.

Therefore, it is clear that Sarah needs more sugar than she already has got. The exact amount of sugar required can be calculated by subtracting total sugar from required sugar. i.e. $0.975 - 0.9375 = 0.0375$

Therefore, Option (c) is correct. $[\frac{3}{80} = 0.0375]$

71. Answer: Option (d)

First find the length of side AB. AB = $\sqrt{(17-5)2 + (8-3)2}$ = 13.
If AB = 13, then A_{square} = 132 = 169.
AB is also the diameter of the circle, so A_{circle} π ($d^2/4$) = 169 π /4.
The area outside the circle, but within the square is:
$A_{square} - A_{circle}$ = 169(1- π /4).

72. Answer: Option (a)

The Pythagorean triple (special right triangle property) means the two shorter sides form a right triangle.
1/2bh = A.
(1/2)(3)(4) = 6.

73. Answer: Option (e)

$AB^2 = AC^2 = AD2 + CD^2$ → $AB^2 = 3^2 + 4^2$ → AB = 5.

74. Answer: Option (a)

In a right triangle, the square of the hypotenuse = the sum of the squares of the other two sides. $AB^2 + BC^2 = AC^2$ → AC^2 = 36 + 64 → AC = 10.

75. Answer: Option (c)

If the area of the square is 36 cm^2, then each side is 6 cm. If we look at the triangle made by half the square, that diagonal would be the hypotenuse of the triangle, and its length = $\sqrt{6^2 + 6}$ ^{2} = $6\sqrt{2}$.
This hypotenuse is also the diameter of the circle, so the radius of the circle is $3\sqrt{2}$.
The area of the circle = $A = \pi r^2$ = 18π.
The area outside the square, but within the circle is 18π -36.

76. Answer: Option (c)

If the area of the square is 25 cm^2, then a side will be 5 cm. If the square is rotated around side AB, which is 5 cm, then the top of the square will sweep a circular area of radius 5 cm to form a three dimensional cylinder. Volume of a cylinder:
$V = \pi * r^2 * h = (5^2) * 5 * \pi = 125\pi$.

77. Answer: Option (b)

Perimeter of a rectangle = 2(l + w).

Width = 5 - x and length = 4(5 - x).

Perimeter = 2(l * w) = 30 → 2(20 - 4x + 5 - x) = 30 → -10x = -20 → x = 2.

78. Answer: Option (a)

If the ratio of AB:AC = 6:10, then this ratio is always constant, regardless of the actual value of AB or AC.

Assuming that AB = 6 and AC = 8, BC = $\sqrt{(AC^2 - AB^2)}$ = 8.

BC:AC = 8:10, which is still a ratio, so it does not matter what the actual values are.

79. Answer: Option (d)

The area of a circle = $\pi * r^2$.

If the diameter is doubled, then the radius is also doubled.

The new area = $\pi * (2r)^2 = 4 * \pi * r^2$. The area increases four times.

80. Answer: Option (a)

Original volume$_{4,5,10}$ = 4 * 5 * 10 = 200 cm^3.

New volume$_{2,10,10}$ = 2 * 10 * 10 = 200 cm^3.

If 1 cm^3 is 30 gm, then 200 cm^3 will be 6000 gm = 6 kg.

81. Answer: Option (b)

The angle of a straight line = 180^0.

$60^0 + 50^0 + \angle A = 180^0$ → $\angle A = 70^0$.

82. Answer: Option (d)

The sum of the three angles of a triangle = 180^0. According to the definition of an isosceles triangle, the two angles that are opposite the two equal sides are also equal. The third angle has to be at least 1^0. The sum of the other two angles = 180-1, or 179^0. Half of 179^0 = 89.5^0.

83. Answer: Option (a)

$\angle A + 25^0 = 180^0$; $\angle A = 155^0$ (Supplementary Angles).

$\angle B = 25^0$ (Corresponding Angles).

$\angle B = \angle C$; $\angle C = 25^0$ (Opposite Angles).

84. Answer: Option (a)

$\angle P = 55^0$. $\angle Q = 90^0$. $\angle R = 180-(55+90) = 35^0$, and $\angle A = 180 - 35 = 145^0$.

85. Answer: Option (c)

$x^2y^3z^5/y^2z^{-9} = x^2y^3z^5 * y^{-2}z^9$ which gives the answer $x^2y^{(3-2)}z^{(5+9)}$ → x^2yz^{14}.

86. Answer: Option (d)

Expand $(2m^3)^5$ to give $32m^{15}$. So $32m^{15} = 32m^{k+1}$ → k+1 = 15 → k = 14.

87. Answer: Option (d)

$x^5y^4z^3/x^{-3}y^2z^{-4} = x^5y^4z^3 * x^3y^{-2}z^4 = x^8y^2z^7$

88. Answer: Option (c)

$(a^2*a^{54}+a^{56}+ (a^{58}/a^2))/a^4 = (a^{54+2}+a^{56}+a^{58-2})a^{-4} = 3a^{56-4} = 3a^{52}$.

89. Answer: Option (d)

9^m is the same as 3^{2m}.

So $3^{2m} = 3^{-1/n}$ → 2m = -1/n → mn = -.5.

90. Answer: Option (e)

$2^a * 4^a$ can be re-written as $2^a * (2^2)^a$.

$32 = 2^5$.

Therefore, $2^{(a+2a)} = 2^5$ → 3a = 5 → a = 5/3.

91. Answer: Option (e)

This evaluates to $\sqrt{3} + 6 + 3 + 4$, or $13+\sqrt{3}$.

92. Answer: Option (d)

If the number is divisible by 2, d should be even. If the number is divisible by 5, then b has to equal 0.

Start by making both variables 0 and dividing by the largest factor, 7.

56800/7 = 8114.

2 from 56800 is 56798, a number divisible by 2 and 7.

Next add a multiple of 7 that turns the last number to a 0. 6 * 7 = 42. 56798 + 42 = 56840, which is divisible by 2, 5 and 7.

93. Answer: Option (e)

We know $(x^2 - 25) = (x + 5)(x - 5)$.

So $(x^2 - 25)/(x + 5) = x - 5$. At x = 0, f(0) = -5.

94. Answer: Option (c)

Replace the value of x with its value and solve the equation.

29 = 5y + 4.

Solving:

29 - 4 = 5y + 4 – 4.

25 = 5y or 5y = 25.

5y/5 = 25/5.

y = 5.

95. Answer: Option (b)

Use FOIL:

$(3x - 4)(6 - 2x) = 3x * 6 - 4 * 6 + 3x * (-2x) - 4 * (-2x) = 18x - 24 - 6x^2 + 8x = -6x^2 + 26x - 24$.

96. Answer: Option (e)

Since $6n + m$ is divisible by 3 and 5, the new number that we get after adding a value will be divisible by 3 and 5 only if the value that we add is divisible by 3 and 5. The only number that will work from the given choices is 60.

97. Answer: Option (e)

We are told $x^3/5 = x/5 \rightarrow x^3 = x$. The possible values are -1, 0, and 1. We are told that x is negative. So $x = -1$.

98. Answer: Option (d)

$30(\sqrt{40} - \sqrt{60}) = 30\sqrt{4(10 - 15)} = 60(\sqrt{10} - \sqrt{15})$

99. Answer: Option (c)

Multiply the numerator and the denominator by $(\sqrt{40} + \sqrt{60})$.

So $30/(\sqrt{40} - \sqrt{60}) * [(\sqrt{40} + \sqrt{60})/(\sqrt{40} + \sqrt{60})] = 30(\sqrt{40} + \sqrt{60})/(\sqrt{40} - \sqrt{60})^2$
$= -3(\sqrt{10} + \sqrt{15})$.

100. Answer: Option (b)

Find all the prime numbers that multiply to give the numbers.

For 2, prime factor is 2; for 3, prime factor is 3; for 4, prime factors are 2, 2; for 5, prime factor is 5. Note the maximum times of occurrence of each prime and multiply these to find the least common multiple. The LCM is $2 * 2 * 3 * 5 = 60$.

Chapter 7: Mechanical Comprehension

The mechanics section of the SIFT has a 15 minute time limit, but the number of questions varies since like the Math Skills Test, it is a computer adaptive section. It is important to note again, you cannot skip any questions, nor can you come back and change any answers. It is imperative that you do your absolute best on each question, meaning that even if you have to guess, carefully eliminate as many wrong choices as possible first.

Before diving into the topics covered in the mechanical section of the SIFT, we should first define two types of values used in physics; **scalars** and **vectors**.

In most basic math, simple numerical values are calculated (for instance 1 + 1 = 2). These simple numbers are known as **scalar** values, meaning they have a magnitude, but no direction, associated with them. Mass is an example of a scalar value commonly used in physics.

However, we live in a three-dimensional universe, so normally a simple number cannot sufficiently describe a physical characteristic. Instead, we need a magnitude as well as a direction, which is known as a **vector**. A vector not only tells how large a value is, but also whether it acts upward, to the left, to the right, etc.

For example, **speed** is a scalar value that tells you how fast an object is going. But if you are driving, knowing only the speed of your car, it will be impossible to navigate. Instead, you need to know your speed as well as the direction in which you are traveling, which is a vector value known as **velocity**. Velocity tells the direction and speed that an object is traveling.

Force and Newton's Laws of Motion

A **force** is a push or pull that can result in an object's motion or change of shape, and has a magnitude and direction, making it a vector. Force is measured in **Newtons** (N) in the metric system of units, but can also be measured in the standard unit of **pounds force** (lbf).

Though its effects can be noticed, a force cannot be seen; it can be thought of as an interaction between two bodies. The basic rules of forces are described by **Newton's Laws of Motion**, which are the foundation of the field of **mechanics.**

1. **First Law of Motion**: Until acted on by an external force, an object's velocity will remain constant, meaning speed and direction will not change. You may recognize: "An object at rest will remain at rest and an object in motion will remain in motion until a force is applied." An object's natural resistance to a change in its motion is known as **inertia**, so Newton's first law is also known as the **Law of Inertia**.

   Intuitively, the law of inertia makes sense. If a soccer ball is resting in a field, it is not going to move until someone kicks it. Once the ball is kicked, though, it does not continue to travel forever, which seems like it is a violation of Newton's first law.

However, there are forces such as drag from the air and friction from the field that eventually cause the ball to come to stop again. In the same way, if a moving car is put into neutral, it will slow down and eventually stop due to parasitic losses in the car's wheels and drivetrain, aero drag, and friction.

2. **Second Law of Motion**: Describes a force's effect on the motion of a body. It states that the acceleration of the object will be proportional to the sum of the forces being applied. Algebraically, Newton's second law is written as: $F = m * a$.

   Here, F is force, m is mass in kilograms (kg) or pounds mass (lbm), and a is acceleration in meters per second squared (m/s^2) or feet per second squared (ft/s^2). Notice that force and acceleration are both vectors, so the acceleration of an object will be in the direction of the force being applied to it.

   Acceleration is defined as the rate of change of an object's velocity. Acceleration does not have to result in a change in speed; it can also cause a change in direction, as is the case in centripetal, or rotational, acceleration. Remember that velocity and acceleration are two separate and distinct values. Just because the acceleration is positive does not mean that the object's velocity is positive and vice versa.

   A negative velocity would mean the object is going backward (or opposite of the direction designated as "positive") and a positive acceleration means the object's velocity is increasing in the positive direction (or decreasing in the negative direction). Though the term "deceleration" is often used to describe a decrease in speed, this is not technically correct. Instead, a change in velocity is always called acceleration and can either be positive or negative, depending on direction.

3. **Third Law of Motion**: Involves the coupling of forces and reactions. The law is often stated as, "For every action there is an equal and opposite reaction." The actions and reactions we are considering are forces. For example, if you lean against a wall, you are applying a force on the wall. According to Newton's third law, the wall is applying the same force back on you. These two forces will be the same magnitude, but in opposite directions; you push toward the wall and the wall pushes back on you. Because there is no motion involved when you lean again a wall, this is considered a **static** example.

   A **dynamic** example of Newton's third law is two cars crashing. If one car collides into a second, stationary car, both cars feel the same amount of force. The force applied to the stationary car is in the direction of the collision and causes the car to begin moving in the same direction as the first car. The moving car would have a force applied to it in the opposite direction by the stationary car, resulting in, among other things, a decrease in speed. Since the force on the two cars will be in opposite directions, the acceleration of the cars will also be in opposite directions; the stationary car speeds up and the moving car slows down.

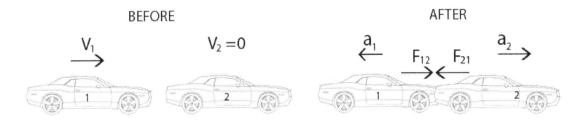

BEFORE   AFTER

V_1 $V_2 = 0$ a_1 F_{12} F_{21} a_2

Collision of a car moving at velocity V_1 into the second stationary car with the force car 1 applies on car 2 F_1, the equal force car 2 applies on car 1 F_{21}, and the resulting accelerations a_1 and a_2.

Centrifugal Force

The terms centripetal and centrifugal force are often incorrectly used interchangeably. A **centripetal force** is a force that makes an object travel along a curved path. This means a centripetal force creates a **centripetal acceleration** toward the center of the curved path.

For example, when a car is driven in a circle, the front tires exert a centripetal force on the car, accelerating it toward the center of the circle. Passengers in the car feel as though they are being pulled toward the outside of the circle, and this pull is **centrifugal acceleration**, which results from **centrifugal force**.

A centrifugal force is the reaction force of a centripetal force that pulls an object toward the outside of the curved path being traveled. This all means that a centrifugal force and a centripetal force are of equal magnitude and opposite directions, just as would be expected of a force and reaction according to Newton's third law. As Newton's second law states, centripetal force equals the mass of the object multiplied by centripetal acceleration:

$$F_c = m * a_c = m * v^2/R$$

Here, a_c is the centripetal acceleration and is equal to the square of the object's linear velocity (v) divided by the radius of the curved path, R.

$$T = Fc = m\frac{v^2}{R}$$

When a ball on a string is swung in a circle, the string exerts a centripetal force on the ball, preventing it from leaving the circular path, and the resulting centrifugal force pulls the ball outward, causing tension in the string and keeping it taut.

The Law of Gravity and Weight

Sir Isaac Newton also formulated the **law of universal gravitation**. Although it is not considered one of Newton's three laws of motion, this is a very important law of physics and has profound implications in our world. Many people are familiar with the story of Isaac Newton observing a falling apple and coming up with the idea of gravity.

Though the authenticity of this story, and even whether Newton was the original formulator of the law, is unclear, Newton's law of universal gravitation is nonetheless named after him, and it describes the mutual attraction between celestial bodies, such as planets and stars. It states that the **gravitational force** two bodies exert on each other is proportional to their masses and inversely proportional to the square of the distance between them:

$$F_g = G * m_1 * m_2 \, r^2$$

Here, G is the **universal gravitation constant** ($6.674 * 10^{-11}$ Nm^2/kg^2), m_1 and m_2 are the masses of the two bodies, and r is the distance between them. You may notice that there is no vector on the right side of this equation. The product of scalar values cannot equal a vector because no direction is specified, so this equation is not technically correct.

This is because the right side of this equation normally has a unit vector with a length of 1 in the direction of the measurement of the distance between the two planets. This has been left out, but remember that gravity is an attractive force; it will always tend to pull two bodies toward each other with equal force.

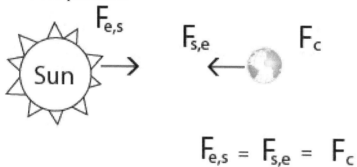

The gravitational force exerted by the sun on the Earth $F_{s,e}$ is equal to the gravitational force applied to the sun by the earth $F_{e,s}$ and is balanced (equal to) the centrifugal force resulting from the Earth's movement.

Newton's law of universal gravitation is a fairly complex concept and would seem difficult to apply to an object on the earth since there are so many objects applying a gravitational force on each other. Just look around; every object you see is applying a gravitational force on you, and you are pulling all those things toward you with the same force!

Thankfully, the law of gravity can be greatly simplified when dealing with objects on the earth's surface. The earth has a mass so much greater than any of the other objects around you that the force of gravity pulling objects toward the earth's center is much stronger than the attraction between any objects on the earth's surface. This means that we can ignore all gravitational forces besides the earth's gravity, which proves accurate when making calculations except in very rare cases, such as when a person is standing next to the

Himalayan Mountains. (Next to the Himalayan Mountains, a plumb line will not point directly toward the center of the earth, but skew slightly toward the mountains, but even in this case the error in measurements is small.)

Another simplification arises from the huge radius of the earth. No matter how good of an arm you have, if you throw a ball into the air, it will not go very far at all when compared to the earth's radius. This means that even if you take an elevator to the top of a very tall building, you really haven't changed your distance from the center of the earth, so you'll still feel approximately the same gravitational force.

Therefore, we can reduce the universal gravitation equation to a simple equation for the earth's force of gravity on an object:

$$F_g = m * g$$

Here, m is the mass of the object in kilograms (kg) or pounds mass (lbm) and g is the **acceleration due to gravity**, which is 9.81 m/s^2 or 32.2 ft/s^2 towards the center of the earth. This constant acceleration of gravity near the surface of the earth means that any object, no matter what its mass, will fall to the ground at the same rate, as long as there is not significant aero drag. If a bowling ball and an orange are dropped from a building at the same time, they will accelerate toward the earth at the same rate and hit the ground at the same time.

The constant acceleration of gravity also gives rise to the concept of **weight**. The weight of an object is merely a measure of the force of gravity on the object ($m * g$), and is measured in Newtons (N) or pounds force (lbf).

The object's mass is a constant scalar value that cannot be changed. However, if the object is taken to another planet, its weight, which is a vector, may be different depending on that planet's acceleration of gravity. The fact that weight is a force means that an object, such as this book, resting on your table exerts a force on the table; the table exerts a force of the same magnitude, the object's weight, back on the object.

This force exerted back on the object opposing the object's weight is known as a **normal force** because it is normal, or perpendicular, to the surface of the table. If you hold this book flat in your hands, you must apply an upward force to keep the book stationary; therefore you are supplying the normal force equal to the book's weight.

Table Supporting the Weight of a Book

Gravity exerts a force equal to the book's weight onto the table and the table exerts an normal force back on the book so the book does not fall to the ground.

Another concept arising from the idea of weight force is an object's **center of gravity** or **center of mass**. The center of mass is essentially the average location of the object and is often used in physics to simplify problems, treating the object as a single particle with all of its mass at its center of gravity.

An object's stability is also determined by the location of its center of gravity. For example, if you stand flat-footed with straight legs and try to reach for an object fairly far in front of you, you may feel off-balanced. When you lean forward and reach out your arms, you are shifting your center of gravity forward in front of your feet, creating a torque that will cause you to fall forward once it is too great for your feet to overcome.

However, if you either bend your knees or stick one of your legs out behind you as you reach forward, the extra weight behind your grounded foot counteracts the weight in front of your foot so that your center of gravity does not shift, keeping you balanced.

This is very similar to a crane that has a large weight just behind the operator's cab to counteract added weight on the crane's arm when lifting. This weight's position is often adjustable, so it can be moved farther away from the crane's base when picking up objects that are either heavy or near the end of the crane's arm; without this large counterweight, a crane could not lift heavy objects without tipping over.

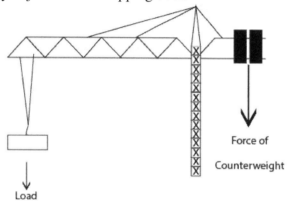

Force of

Counterweight

Load

Torque
Torque (twisting force which attempts to rotate an object), or **moment** due to a force, equals the distance of the force from the **fulcrum**, or pivot point, multiplied by the tangential force: $T = F * r$.

F is the force and r is the **torque arm**, or distance from the fulcrum.

In the crane example, the middle of the crane acts as a fulcrum and the counterweight and load apply forces downward, creating two moments in opposite directions; the load is twisting the crane counterclockwise and the counterweight twists clockwise. Torque is measured in Newton-meters (Nm) or foot-pounds-force (lbf-ft).

It is important to remember that the force and distance are both vectors, which means that the component of force and the torque arm considered must be perpendicular. Applying force to the handle of a wrench is another example.

If the 10lbf force is applied to a 10-inch wrench, then the torque on the bolt is 100 in-lbf. If the force is not applied at a 90 degree angle, the resulting torque will not be as high. For instance, if the force is applied at a 30 degree angle to the wrench handle, then the component of the force perpendicular to the wrench is only 5 lbf, and the resulting torque is just 50 in-lbf.

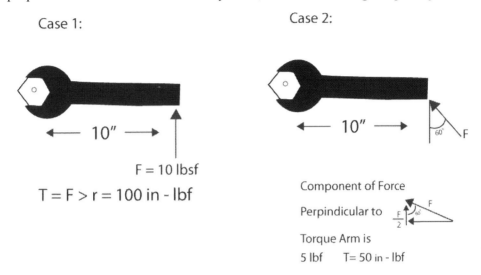

Case 1:

F = 10 lbsf

T = F > r = 100 in - lbf

Case 2:

Component of Force

Perpindicular to

Torque Arm is

5 lbf   T= 50 in - lbf

Friction

The normal force created by gravity also gives rise to a resistance to sliding known as **friction**. If you try to slide a refrigerator across a floor, you may find it very hard to move the object. Newton's third law suggests that there must be a force opposing your attempts to push the refrigerator; if not, it would easily slide across the floor and continue to slide until acted on by another force, such as a wall. This force opposing your efforts to move the refrigerator is friction. There are two types of friction: static and kinetic.

As you might have guessed, **static friction** is the force of friction between two objects that are not moving relative to each other. Static friction arises from the attempt to slide two surfaces past each other. In our refrigerator example, there is no force of friction until you attempt to push the refrigerator.

If you are not applying a force on the refrigerator, the only forces felt by the refrigerator are the force of gravity and the normal force of the floor holding it up, both of which are equal to the refrigerator's weight. When you start to push on the refrigerator and it does not move, static friction is holding the refrigerator in place.

The force of static friction is equal to the force that you are applying to the refrigerator; however, once pushed hard enough, the refrigerator will begin to move. The force necessary to start sliding an object is called **stiction** and is given by the equation: $F_{f,s} = \mu_s * N$.

$F_{f,s}$ is the maximum force of static friction (stiction), N is the normal force applied on the object by the surface across which it is sliding, and μ_s is the **coefficient of static friction**. Past this stiction point, the object will begin to move, and the force of **kinetic friction** will oppose the sliding motion: $F_{f,k} = \mu_k * N$. This is the same as the equation for static friction, except that the coefficient μ_k is the **coefficient of kinetic friction**.

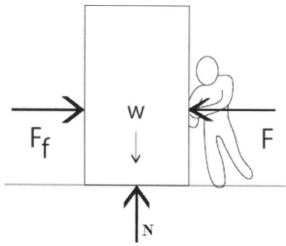

The force of friction, whether static or kinetic, will always oppose the direction of the force causing the sliding. Also, both coefficients of friction are always less than one, and the coefficient of static friction is usually greater than the coefficient of kinetic friction.

This means that it takes a greater force to get an object to start sliding across a surface than it does to keep the object sliding once it has already started. The figure following shows a graph of the force of friction versus the sliding force applied to an object.

Considering this graph in relation to our refrigerator example, if you start pushing on the refrigerator, the force of static friction will prevent sliding until you have applied enough force to overcome the stiction point. After this, the force of kinetic friction will give a constant opposition to the sliding, no matter how hard or fast you push.

Force of Friction (F_f) with Increasing Applied Force (F)

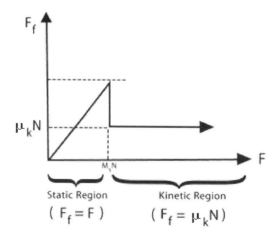

Energy

An object raised to a height above the ground will have an amount of stored energy known as **gravitational potential energy**. The higher an object is moved, the more potential it has. Gravitational potential energy is defined as: $PE = m * g * h$.

Here, m is the mass of the object, g is the acceleration of gravity (9.81 m/s^2), and h is the height of the object from the surface of the earth.

Sometimes, gravitational potential energy is represented by the letter U instead of PE.

Gravitational potential energy, like all types of energy, is given in units of joules (J) or foot-pounds-force (ft-lbf). You may notice that gravitational potential energy is simply the force of gravity on an object multiplied by the objects height.

Since the force of gravity, or weight, is given in units of Newtons, one joule is the same as one Newton multiplied by one meter ($1J = 1Nm$). When an object is dropped, its gravitational potential energy is converted into **kinetic energy**, which is defined as: $KE = ½ m * v^2$.

Here, m is again the mass of the object and v is the object's velocity.

Kinetic energy also has units of joules and is sometimes represented by the letter E instead of KE. Energy is always conserved, meaning it cannot be created or destroyed. This is known as the law of **conservation of energy**. The law of conservation of gravitational energy can be written as:
$PE + KE = m * g * h + ½ m * v^2 = $ constant.

However, all types of energy are always conserved, whether mechanical, electrical, chemical, nuclear, solar, etc. Even the power plants that supply our homes with electricity do not create energy; they simply convert kinetic, chemical, nuclear, or solar energy into electrical energy.

If an object is brought to a certain height, it has a particular amount of gravitational potential energy. When the object is dropped, its potential energy is converted to kinetic energy, so the amount of gravitational potential energy that the object had at its highest point will be exactly how much kinetic energy it has as it hits the ground (ignoring aero drag).

The law of conservation of energy applies to all objects in a gravitational field, so the velocity of a falling object will depend only on the height through which it has fallen and not the path. This means that the same laws used to find the speed of a falling baseball can also be used to find the speed of a rollercoaster.

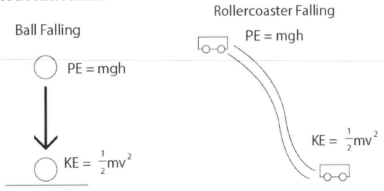

151

Work

In physics, the term **work** refers to a force applied over some distance: $W = F * d$.

F is the force being applied, and d is the distance of movement in the direction of the force.

It is important to remember that the distance measured is the **displacement** in the direction of the force, which is not the same as total distance traveled; displacement is the distance between the starting and ending points.

If you are holding a book and either keep it stationary or move it to the side, no work has been accomplished because you are pushing upward on the book and there has been no upward movement.

If you move the book upward, work has been done against gravity, and if you allow the book to move downward while holding it, you have done negative work because the movement was opposite the direction of the force you are applying.

In the case of downward movement, one can also say that gravity has done the work; the gravitational force is pulling the book downward in the same direction as the book's movement, so gravity has done positive work on the book.

Work is given in units of joules (J) or foot-pounds-force (ft-lbf). This is the same unit as energy because work can also be thought of as a change in the state of energy of an object, known as the **work-energy theorem**.

In our example of the book, if it weighs 1N and you lift it 1m upward, you have done 1 J of work, or added 1 J of gravitational potential energy. You can verify this by comparing the equations for work and potential energy. Since the force you are exerting to hold up the book is equal to the weight of the book, the work equation is the same as the equation for gravitational potential energy ($m * g * h$).

Power

Power is the rate at which work is done: $P = W/t$.

W is the amount of work done in joules (J) and t is the time over which the work was accomplished in seconds (s). One joule per second (J/s) is equal to a watt (W), the common metric unit of power.

Power can also be given in units of foot-pounds-force per second (ft-lbf/s) or horsepower (hp). One horsepower is equal to 550 ft-lb/s or 746 W. Work is force times distance, so if a force is being applied to an object to move it at a constant velocity, we can also say that power is force times velocity:
$P = F * d/t = F * v$.

F is force, and v is velocity either in meters per second (m/s) or feet per second (ft/s).

Simple Machines

These physics definitions of work and power can be counterintuitive. If you hold dumbbells in front of you with your arms outstretched, you will eventually grow tired. However, if the weights are not moving, according to the laws of physics, no work has been done and, no matter how long you hold the weights, no power will ever be used. Your physical exhaustion results not from the work done, but the force you have to apply to hold the weights in place.

This is the basis for the simple machines that we use to make our lives easier every day. **Simple machines** are devices that change the direction or magnitude of a force. The **mechanical advantage** of simple machine is defined as the output force divided by the force that is applied: $MA = F_{out}/F_{in}$.

F_{out} is the machine's output force or load and F_{in} is the force input or effort to the simple machine. The mechanical advantage is, in a sense, the percentage of the input force that is applied as the output of the simple machine. A simple machine does not do work or create power, instead work and power are said to be conserved, meaning that a simple machine can multiply force only by sacrificing displacement and speed.

Levers

The first type of simple machine we will look at is the lever. A **lever** is simply a beam with a pivot or hinge known as a **fulcrum**, which can either multiply the input force by sacrificing output travel distance or multiply distance and speed with a decreased output force. The mechanical advantage of lever is given by: $MA_{lever} = d_{in}/d_{out}$.

Here, d_{in} is the distance from the fulcrum to the point where the input force is applied, or input arm, and d_{out} is the output arm, or distance from the fulcrum to the point of the output force. Levers are divided into three types or classes: **first class**, **second class**, and **third class**.

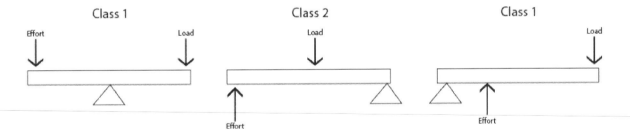

When an input force is applied to a lever, it creates a moment, or torque, about the fulcrum, which is then balanced by the output force. This means the input force multiplied by the input arm is equal to the output force multiplied by the output arm.

1. **First Class Lever**: The fulcrum is between the input and output forces, which are in opposite directions. A popular example of a first class lever is a seesaw. On a seesaw, when one person is in the air, their weight is applying a downward force on one end of the lever and the other person must apply an upward force to bring

them back to the earth. A seesaw has input and output arms of equal length, so the mechanical advantage is one, meaning the input and output force and the distances traveled by the two riders are equal.

A first class lever like this is said to have no mechanical advantage, or a mechanical advantage of one, because it merely changes the direction of the input force. If it is desired to multiply the input force, the input arm should be lengthened. This will give the lever a mechanical advantage greater than one.

Conversely, by lengthening the input arm, the output force will not move as far. If the output arm is longer, it will move faster and farther than the input arm, but a greater input force is required. A lever like this would have a mechanical advantage less than one.

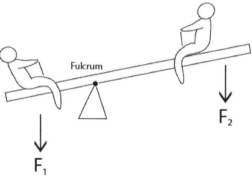

2. **Second Class Lever**: The input and output forces are on the same side of the fulcrum, with the output force closer to the fulcrum, meaning that a second class lever will always have a mechanical advantage greater than one. The most popular example of a second class lever is a wheelbarrow. The front wheel of a wheelbarrow acts as its fulcrum and the user lifts far behind the location of the load in order to lift very heavy objects.

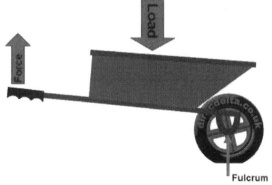

3. **Third Class Lever**: The input and output forces are on the same side of the fulcrum on a **third class lever** as well. In contrast to a second class lever, the input force of a third class lever is applied closer to the fulcrum than the load.

This means third class levers have a mechanical advantage less than one and are used to increase the output distance or speed. For example, take a swinging baseball bat: The batter places both hands near the end of the handle and swings; the top hand moves faster than the other, so the slower hand acts as a fulcrum. The end which makes contact with the ball is moving very quickly when the ball is hit.

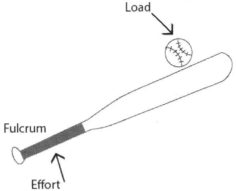

Inclined Planes

The **inclined plane** is another simple machine. Basic inclined planes are often used to do work against gravity, as is the case with a ramp. When an inclined plane is used to move an object upward, the user does not have to use as much force as if they lifted the object vertically upward.

However, the user must apply the force over a greater distance, so the work required is the same for both cases if we ignore friction. The mechanical advantage of an inclined plane is: $MA_{\text{inclined plane}} = L/H$.

L is the length of the inclined plane and H is the height, as shown in the figure below. This equation can be confusing when compared to our original mechanical advantage equation ($MA = F_{out}/F_{in}$), but in the case of an inclined plane, we can think of the output force as the force required if the load were lifted vertically upward, and the input force as the actual effort required when using the inclined plane.

It would seem that the most efficient inclined plane would have an extremely long length because this increases the mechanical advantage. However, increasing the length not only increases the travel distance up the ramp but also the strength requirement of the plane. This is similar to breaking a stick by bending it. If you have a very long twig, it can be easily broken in half.

Once the stick has been broken in half, the shorter resulting halves will be harder to break. If the process is repeated a few times, you may no longer be able to break the stick by hand. When an inclined plane is used to lift a load, the item being lifted applies a downward force to the ramp, bending and possibly breaking it if the ramp is too long or weak.

 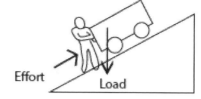

Inclined Plane

Screws

A **screw** is a specific application of the inclined plane; it is simply an inclined plane wrapped around a cylinder. If you look closely at a single-threaded screw, a triangle can be formed out of the threading by connecting consecutive teeth. The mechanical advantage of the screw will depend on the length of the tool used to turn the screw.

A screw can also be used for lifting heavy objects with the setup shown below, known as a **screw jack**. The mechanical advantage for this assembly is: $MA_{\text{screw jack}} = 2\pi R/P$.

Here, R is the torque arm, or distance from the center of the bolt (the fulcrum) and P is the distance between two consecutive teeth on the screw threading, known as the thread's pitch.

This mechanical advantage is found by considering the total distance that the input force must travel ($2\pi R$) and the total height that the screw will rise (P) in one turn of the input torque arm. Sometimes the mechanical advantage of only the screw is given, without specifying a tool or setup used to turn the screw.
In these cases, the radius of the shaft around which the inclined plane is wrapped is used as the torque arm r in the mechanical advantage equation.

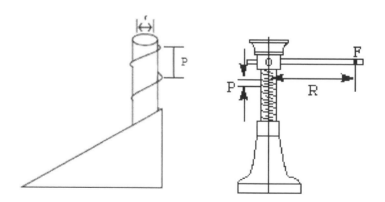

Wedges

The **wedge** is another variation of the inclined plane. A wedge can be thought of as two inclined planes placed back-to-back. Wedges are normally used for cutting and splitting as well as securing an object in place. An axe or knife is an example of a wedge used for cutting or splitting. A wedge is also used to secure the head of a hammer to its handle and to hold

156

open doors as a doorstop. The mechanical advantage equation of a wedge differs only slightly from that for an inclined plane: $MA_{wedge} = L/t$.

The thickness, t, is measured across the end of the wedge. Again, it would seem that a wedge should be as long and sharp as possible, but a thinner, sharper wedge not only is transversely weaker (to side-loading), but also has a tendency of binding when used to chop. For instance, if a log-splitting axe is too sharp, it can become lodged in the wood with the log flexing back onto the blade, increased friction and making the axe difficult to remove.

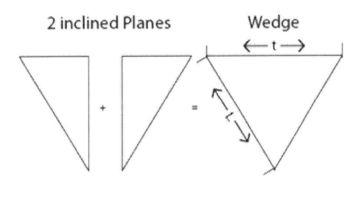

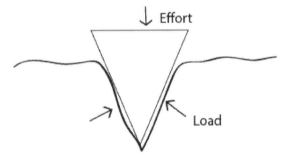

An Axe (Wedge) Splitting Wood

Pulleys and the Block and Tackle
The next type of simple machine we'll look at is the **pulley**. Pulleys are not used alone; they are used to support a cable, rope, belt, or chain, so we should discuss these items, which we will refer to simply as "cords" from now on, before trying to understand pulleys. Cords can be thought of simply as force transmitters.

However, unlike solid bodies and fluids, cords can only transmit pulling force, known as **tension**. If you try to bend or push on a cord it flexes, providing no resistance; if you secure a cord to an object and pull on it, though, it will transmit this pull as tension to the object to which it is attached.

When loaded, the tension throughout a cord is uniform, meaning that every piece of a cord along its length sees the exact same load. This is where the phrase, "A chain is only as strong as its weakest link" comes from. Each link in the chain will see the same load and be under the same amount of stress, so the entire chain can only hold the amount that the weakest link can hold before breaking.

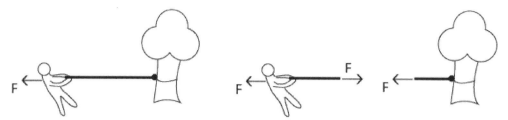

When you pull on a rope, the force is uniformly distributed through
the length of the rope as tension.

A **pulley** is a wheel and axle that supports a cord and, in doing so, changes the direction of cord's orientation and therefore the direction of the tension in the cord. Although pulleys have some frictional losses, they are small enough that we can ignore them and say that the tension in the cord is uniform. This means that the pulling force's direction is changed while its magnitude stays the same. This means that a single pulley offers no mechanical advantage ($F_{in} = F_{out}$ so $MA_{pulley} = 1$).

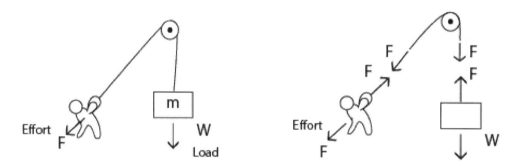

When a pulley is used to suspend an object, the tension in the rope is
uniform and equal to the weight of the object.

However, a series of pulleys, known as a block and tackle, can be used to give a mechanical advantage and make it possible to more easily lift heavy objects. When the input force is applied to a single cord, the mechanical advantage of a block and tackle can be found by counting the number of cord segments whose tension is being applied to lift the object: $MA_{b\&t} = N$.

Here, N is the number of cord segments extending from the moving output block, as shown in the pictures below. Again, this mechanical advantage comes at the cost of moving distance, so if the mechanical advantage is 4, then the output block will only move one quarter of the distance traveled by the input force.

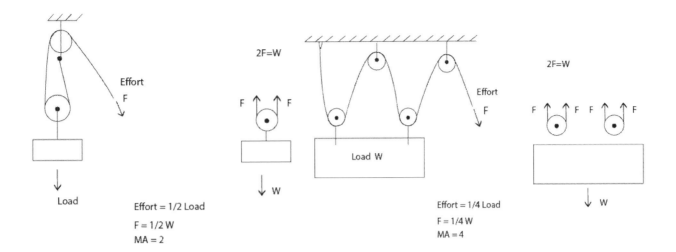

2F=W

Effort
F

Load

Effort = 1/2 Load
F = 1/2 W
MA = 2

2F=W

Effort
F

F   F
F   F

Load W

Effort = 1/4 Load
F = 1/4 W
MA = 4

2F=W

F   F   F   F

W

The Wheel and Axle

We said that a pulley is a wheel and axle, but the wheel and axle is, in its own right, a simple machine. **Wheel and axle** refers to two cylinders that are attached to each other coaxially that are allowed to rotate about their center, as shown below. The wheel and axle can be thought of as a variation of the lever, with the fulcrum at the center and the forces applied tangentially to the surface of the wheel and the axle, sometimes using belts or rope wrapped around the wheel and/or axle. In this way, the wheel and axle creates a continuous lever. The mechanical advantage of a wheel and axle assembly is given by:

$$MA_{w\&a} = R_{wheel}/R_{axle}$$

Here, R_{wheel} and R_{axle} are the radii of the wheel and axle, respectively.

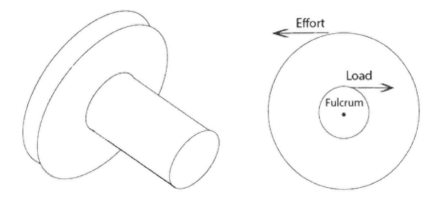

Effort

Load

Fulcrum

However, an axle does not have to have only one wheel and each wheel does not have to be the same size. The wheels on a car are the same size, but sometimes wheel and axles are required to turn various machine parts at different speeds. For this, assemblies like the one shown below are necessary. The mechanical advantage between two different wheels can be found as: $MA_{wheels} = R_{in}/R_{out.}$

Here, R_{in} and R_{out} are the radii of the input wheel and output wheel, respectively. The mechanical advantage of the wheel and axle and two-wheel assembly are both found by comparing the input and output moments about the axis; the input and output torques must be

159

equal. Remember again that this mechanical advantage will be gained by sacrificing the distance traveled.

For instance, if the input wheel has a radius four times as large as the output, the mechanical advantage will be four. This means the output force will be four times as large as the input, but the circumference of the output wheel is a quarter of that of the input wheel, so a belt attached to the output wheel will turn only a quarter as far as one attached to the input wheel.

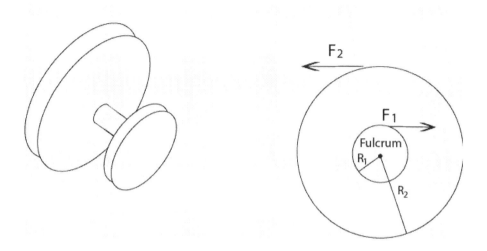

Gears

The rotation and torque of a wheel can be transmitted a great distance by connecting two wheels with a belt or chain, as shown below The mechanical advantage of this setup is given by: $MA_{gears} = R_{out} / R_{in}$.

R_{out} and R_{in} are again the output and input radii, respectively. Notice that this mechanical advantage is the inverse of the mechanical advantage between two wheels on the same axle (MA_{wheels}) and is denoted as MA_{gears}. The reason that a belt or chain assembly's mechanical advantage is represented by MA_{gears} is that this type of pulley assembly is the same basic concept as two gears; it is two disks rotating with the same tangential velocity at their contact point.

However, two gears will rotate in opposite directionsThe only major difference between two meshed gears and two pulleys connected by a belt or chain is that two consecutive gears will rotate in opposite directions while the pulleys connected by a belt or chain will rotate in the same diection. **Gears** are simply interlocking wheels with their **effective radii** given by the point at which the two wheels have the same velocity.

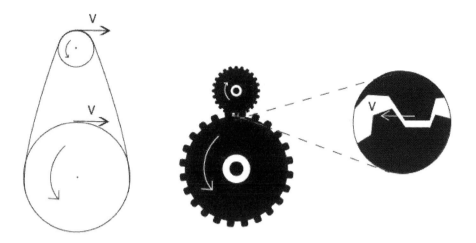

Effective radii at two gears are given by the point at which their linear velocities are equal. Pulleys connected by a belt or chain are two discs that turn with the same velocity at their radii, just like gears, and the assembly's mechanical advantage is calculated the same way as a pair of gears.

However, a pair of gears will rotate in opposite directions.

To find the mechanical advantage of a long **gear train**, or series of gears interlocked together, we only need to worry about the input and output gear radii, not the radii of the gears in between, as long as they are interlocked and not on the same shaft.

Again, if the output gear has a radius four times that of the input gear, the mechanical advantage will be four but the output gear will only rotate once for every four rotations of the input gear.

For two interlocking gears, the force applied at the effective radius, or meshing point, is the same for both gears, similar to the tension being constant throughout a rope or belt in the pulley assemblies. Since the gears are different radii, this creates different moments on the two gears. If the input gear is driving a larger output gear, the output force is greater than the input and the assembly is called a torque-multiplier or speed-reduction assembly. If the output gear is smaller than the input, the assembly is a speed-multiplying or torque-reducing assembly.

$$MA = \frac{Ru}{R3} \; x \frac{R3}{R2} \; x \; \frac{R2}{R1} \; = \; \frac{R4}{R1} = \; \frac{R\,out}{R\,in}$$

161

Fluids and Hydraulics

If a force needs to be transmitted a great distance, it may not be convenient to use any of the mechanical simple machines discussed above. Instead, fluids can be used to transmit the force through hydraulic and pneumatic systems. The term fluid is not synonymous with liquid. A **fluid** is any material that conforms to the shape of its container and is not compressible, so we consider any liquid or gas to be an incompressible fluid.

In fluids, we define **pressure** as a force per unit area, given in pounds per square inch (psi); Pascals (Pa), which is the equivalent of one Newton (N) per square meter (m^2); or **inches of mercury** (in Hg), which is defined as the pressure exerted by a one-inch high column of liquid mercury.

The principle of transmission of pressure, also known as **Pascal's law**, states that pressure applied to one part of the fluid will be distributed evenly to the entire rest of the fluid. In large containers of liquid, the pressure relies on the pressure applied at the surface as well as the depth within the container, so the pressure increases deeper in the container due to the weight of the water.

However, in containers of gas or shallow containers of liquids, the effects of gravity can be ignored and the pressure is constant throughout the container. This principle is utilized in **hydraulics** through the setup shown in the picture below.

In this simplified hydraulic system, one piston is applying a pressure that is equal to the input force spread over the area of the piston's face. This pressure is distributed throughout the fluid, so the face of the second piston will see the same force per unit area. This relationship is stated mathematically as:

$$P_{in} = P_{out}$$
$$F_{in} / A_{in} = F_{out} / A_{out}$$

P_{in} is the pressure on the face of the input piston, which is the input force divided by the area of the input piston's face and is equal to the output pressure P_{out}. Since the output piston in this case is larger, the output force will be greater. For this dual-piston setup, we can define a mechanical advantage by dividing the output force by the input (the definition of mechanical advantage): $MA_{pistons} = A_{out} / A_{in.}$

Remember, this mechanical advantage is gained through decreasing the output motion, so if the output piston has an area four times that of the input, the mechanical advantage will be four, so the output force will be four times the input; however, the output piston will only move a quarter of the distance of the input piston's travel, assuming incompressibility of the fluid.

162

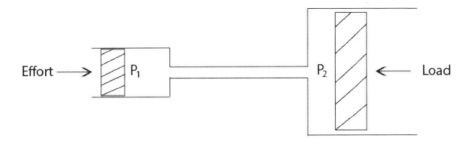

Basic Piston setup of Hydraulic System
The input force is distributed over the face of the input piston and transferred
to the fluid as pressure, which is applies an output force to the second piston.

This difference in piston motion can also be explained by considering volume displacement of the fluid. When the input piston moves, it displaces a volume of fluid equal to the area of the piston multiplied by the distance of the piston's motion.

This volume displaced causes the output piston to move to make room for the volume entering the cylinder, but since the output piston has a larger area, it will not need to move as far to displace the same amount of fluid.

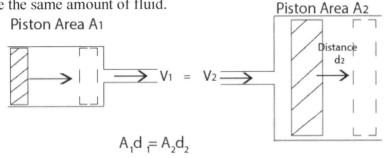

The movement of the pistons in the hydraulic system can also be explained
by fluid displacement. The volume of fluid displaced by the movement of
the first piston ($V_1=A_1d_1$) flows into the second cylinder ($V_1=V_2$) and
causes the piston to move to make room for the incoming fluid.

This volume displacement concept can also be applied to a fluid flowing through a pipe. When a fluid is flowing through a pipe, mass must be conserved, meaning that no amount of fluid is gathering anywhere in the pipe; the amount of fluid flowing into the pipe is equal to the amount flowing out.

Since the flow is constant through all points in the pipe, the flow velocity must increase whenever the cross-sectional area of the pipe decreases. Mathematically, the law of **conservation of mass** is stated as:

$$Q_1 = Q_2$$
$$v_1 * A_1 = v_2 * A_2$$

Here, Q_1 and Q_2 are the volumetric flow rates of the fluid, v_1 and v_2 are the velocities of fluid particles, and A_1 and A_2 are the cross-sectional areas of the pipe at points 1 and 2, respectively.

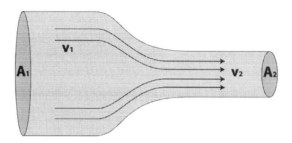

Energy must also be conserved in the flow of a fluid, just like any other body subjected to gravity. Unlike solid bodies, however, fluids also have a defined pressure energy. This means that between any two points, the sum of a fluid's pressure, kinetic, and potential energies must remain constant. Mathematically, this is stated in a force per unit area basis:

$$p + \tfrac{1}{2}\rho v^2 + \rho g h = \text{constant}$$
$$p_1/\rho + v_1^2/2 + g\,h_1 = p_2/\rho + v_2^2/2 + g\,h_2$$

Here, p is pressure, ρ is the density of the fluid (which we assume remains constant), v is the velocity of the fluid, g is the acceleration of gravity (9.81 m/s^2 or 32.2 ft/s^2), and h is the height of the fluid.

This relationship is known as **Bernoulli's principle** and can be applied to any points along a streamline. A **streamline** is an imaginary line through a smoothly flowing fluid that is always tangential to the fluid's velocity, and can be thought of as a line that would follow the path of a particle flowing through the fluid.

Practice Drill: Mechanical Comprehension

1. A person moves forward ten steps and then backwards ten steps. What is the total distance traveled?
    a) -10 steps.
    b) 0 steps.
    c) 10 steps.
    d) 20 steps.

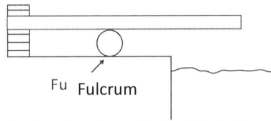

2. A springboard is a diving board made out of a flexible platform that acts like a spring and is held stationary by a hinge on one end with an adjustable fulcrum, so that a person can dive off the other end, as shown in the picture above. What will happen if the fulcrum is moved away from the diver?
    a) The board will be stiffer.
    b) The board will flex more under the weight of the diver.
    c) Fulcrum position makes no difference.
    d) The platform will be less likely to break.

3. A car travels 60 miles south in one hour, and then 90 miles north in two hours. What is the total displacement during this time?
    a) -30 miles.
    b) 0 miles.
    c) 30 miles.
    d) 150 miles.

4. For the car described in problem #3, what is the average speed during the first hour of travel?
    a) -60 mph.
    b) 1 mph.
    c) 50 mph.
    d) 60 mph.

5. For the car described in problem #3, what is the average speed during the 3 hours of travel?
    a) -10 mph.
    b) 0 mph.
    c) 10 mph.
    d) 50 mph.

6. For the car in problem #3, what is the average velocity during the 3 hours of travel, if we define north as the positive direction?
   a) -10 mph.
   b) -1 mph.
   c) 1 mph.
   d) 10 mph.

7. A 10 kg person stands on a scale. Approximately what will the scale read?
   a) 10 N.
   b) 32 N.
   c) 98 N.
   d) 196 N.

8. A 10 kg person travels to the Moon, which has a smaller acceleration due to gravity than the Earth. What will happen to the person's mass?
   a) The person's mass will decrease.
   b) The person's mass will stay the same.
   c) The person's mass will increase.
   d) It is impossible to tell from this information.

9. A 10 kg person travels to the Moon, which has a smaller acceleration due to gravity than the Earth. What will happen to the person's weight?
   a) The person's weight will decrease.
   b) The person's weight will stay the same.
   c) The person's weight will increase.
   d) It is impossible to tell from this information.

10. A person travels to a distant planet and finds that their weight has increased relative to their weight on Earth. Assuming the person's mass has not changed, what can we say about the planet's radius?
   a) The planet's radius is smaller than that of Earth.
   b) The planet's radius is equal to that of the Earth.
   c) The planet's radius is larger than that of the Earth.
   d) It is impossible to tell from this information.

11. What force is required to accelerate a 10 kg object from rest to 10 m/s in 5 seconds? (Assume no resistive forces.)
   a) 15 N.
   b) 20 N.
   c) 100 N.
   d) 500 N.

12. A 50 kg object begins at rest on a surface with a static coefficient of friction at 0.6 and a kinetic coefficient of friction at 0.5. If you push horizontally on the object with a force of 27 N, how quickly will it move across the surface? (Assume that the object does not tip over.)
- a) 0 m/s.
- b) 5 m/s.
- c) 20 m/s.
- d) 30 m/s.

13. Which of these best describes the gear train above?
- a) Torque-multiplier.
- b) Speed-multiplier.
- c) Frequency-multiplier.
- d) None of the above.

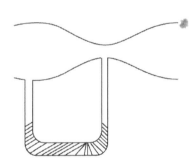

14. The figure above shows an air duct that narrows at a point. A U-tube is attached as shown and the bottom is filled with water. What will happen to the water when air starts flowing through the duct?
- a) The left side will go up and the right side will go down.
- b) Both sides will go down.
- c) The left side will go down and the right side will go up.
- d) Both sides will go up.

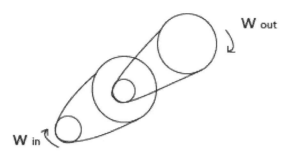

15. Which of these describes the pulley train shown above?
    a) Rotation-inverter.
    b) Speed-multiplier.
    c) Torque-multiplier.
    d) None of the above.

16. To have the best leverage in the scissors above, you should:
    a) Hold the scissors at D and cut at A.
    b) Hold the scissors at D and cut at B.
    c) Hold the scissors at C and cut at A.
    d) Hold the scissors at C and cut at B.

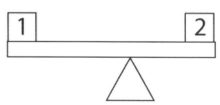

17. Which of the objects in the picture above weighs more?
    a) Object 1.
    b) Object 2.
    c) They weigh the same amount.
    d) It is impossible to tell.

18. Which of these statements is true about a car's transmission?
   a) Higher gears have a higher mechanical advantage.
   b) Lower gears have a higher mechanical advantage.
   c) All the gears have the same mechanical advantage.
   d) The mechanical advantage depends on the weight of the car.

19. In the picture above, does the support on the left or right carry more of the object's weight?
   a) Left supports more weight.
   b) Right supports more weight.
   c) They carry the same amount of weight.
   d) It is impossible to tell.

20. Three cubes of equal volume are put in a hot oven. The cubes are made of three materials: wood, iron, and silver. Which cube will heat the fastest?
   a) The wooden cube.
   b) The iron cube.
   c) The silver cube.
   d) The cubes all heat up at the same rate.

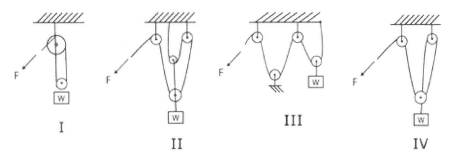

21. Which of block and tackle pictured above requires the least effort to lift a weight of W?
   a) I.
   b) II.
   c) III.
   d) IV.

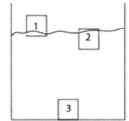

22. What can be said about the three objects shown above in a tank of water?
    a) Object 3 weighs the most.
    b) Object 1 has the lowest density.
    c) Objects 1 and 2 have the same density.
    d) None of the above.

23. Two gears create a mechanical advantage of 4:1 and the larger gear has 24 teeth. How many teeth does the pinion have?
    a) 6 teeth.
    b) 12 teeth.
    c) 24 teeth.
    d) 96 teeth.

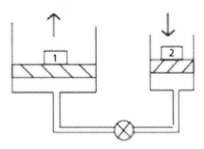

24. In the hydraulic system shown above, the valve is originally closed and the two objects are level. When the valve is opened, the object on the right begins to move downward and the object on the left moves upward. What can be said about the two objects?
    a) Object 1 weighs more.
    b) Object 2 weighs more.
    c) The objects weigh the same amount.
    d) It is impossible to tell from this information.

25. The figure above is a simplified model of the camshaft in a car's engine. The pulley attached to the crankshaft is of half the diameter of the pulley attached to the camshaft. About how far must the crankshaft turn before the camshaft pushes the valve all the way open?

    a) 90 degrees.
    b) 180 degrees.
    c) 270 degrees.
    d) 540 degrees.

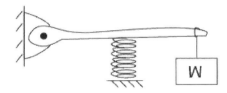

26. The picture above shows a hinged arm attached to a weight and being held horizontal by a spring. If the weight is moved to the left (closer to the hinge), what will happen?

    a) The spring will compress more.
    b) The spring will extend.
    c) Nothing.
    d) It is impossible to tell.

27. The picture above shows an axe splitting a piece of wood. What type of simple machine is this?

    a) Lever.
    b) Blade.
    c) Inclined plane.
    d) None of these.

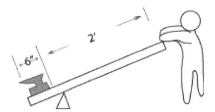

28. The picture above shows a person lifting a heavy object with a lever. What is the mechanical advantage?
- a) 0.25.
- b) 0.3.
- c) 3.
- d) 4.

29. Which of these best describes the gear train shown above?
- a) Torque-multiplier.
- b) Speed-multiplier.
- c) Frequency-multiplier.
- d) None of the above.

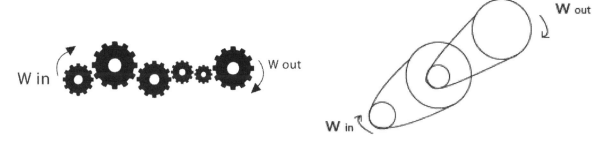

30. If the input gear on the left has the same diameter as the input pulley on the right and the output gear on the left has the same diameter as the output pulley on the right, which assembly gives the higher mechanical advantage?
- a) The gear train on the left.
- b) The pulley train on the right.
- c) The assemblies have the same mechanical advantage.
- d) It is impossible to tell.

Practice Drill: Mechanical Comprehension – Answers

1. **d) 20 steps**. Total distance traveled does not take direction into account, so we can add the two distances: $10 + 10 = 20$ steps.

2. **b) The board will flex more under the weight of the diver**. The distance between the fulcrum and the diver is being lengthened, so the torque arm is being increased; the weight of the diver will apply a greater moment to the platform, resulting in the platform flexing a greater amount.

   You can also consider the two extremes of the fulcrum either being adjusted directly underneath the diver or as far away from the diver as possible. If the fulcrum is underneath the diver the board will not flex at all, and if the fulcrum is the farthest point away from the diver the board will flex the maximum amount.

   This means that the board flexes more as the fulcrum is adjusted away from the diver. Since the board is flexing more, it would be more likely to break because there is a greater moment.

3. **c) 30 miles**. Displacement is the distance between the starting and ending points, so we cannot simply add the two distances together. If we take north as the positive direction, the car moves 60 miles in the positive direction and then 90 miles in the negative direction.

   Adding these values, $60+ (-90) = 60 – 90 = -30$ miles. However, displacement is always positive. Displacement is not a vector, but a scalar. It is just the distance between the start and end points, NOT the vector distance between the two points.

4. **d) 60 mph**. Speed is distance traveled divided by time and does not take direction into account. In this case, the car travels 60 miles in one hour, 60 miles / 1 hour = 60 miles per hour.

5. **d) 50 mph**. Speed is a scalar value, so it does not take direction into account. Average speed is distance traveled divided by time (x/t), so we first find the distance traveled, $60 + 90 = 150$ miles, then the total time, $1 + 2 = 3$ hours, and finally divide the distance by time, $150/3 = 50$ miles per hour.

   While it is also possible to find the average speed during the two legs of the trip and calculate a weighted average, this is much more complicated and reduces to the same equation.

6. **d) 10 mph**. Notice in this question we have to define a positive direction because the question asks for a vector value, which has a magnitude and direction. Similar to problem #4, we must first find the total displacement of the car, which is 30 miles. Remember that this is north, which has been defined as the positive direction.

Like average speed, average velocity is distance divided by time, 30 miles/3 hours = 10 mph, and since the distance traveled is in the positive direction, the average velocity will also be positive: +30/3 = +10mph.-30

Again, we could also find the average velocity during each leg of the trip and find a weighted average, but this is even more complicated when working with vector values and still reduces to the same equation of total distance divided by total time.

7. **c) 98 N**. A scale measures weight, and since it is the earth's gravitational pull on the object which is being weighed, the force of gravity is the mass of the object times the constant acceleration due to gravity (9.8 m/s^2). W = mg = 10 * 9.8 = 98 N

8. **b) The person's mass will stay the same**. Mass is a scalar vector depends on the density and volume of an object, both of which will stay constant. A person's mass will stay the same no matter what planet they are on.

9. **a) The person's weight will decrease**. Weight is a measurement of force, so it is a vector value which has a magnitude that depends on mass and acceleration. We already found in problem #8 that the person's mass will not change, so their weight will be proportional to the acceleration of gravity.

   Since the acceleration due to gravity on the moon is less than that of the earth, the acceleration of gravity will decrease when the person travels to the moon, meaning their weight will also decrease.

10. **d) It is impossible to tell from this information**. Since the person's weight has increased, the acceleration of gravity on this distant planet is higher than that on Earth. It is tempting to say this must be a smaller planet. However, we cannot say anything about the planet's radius because gravitational force depends on both the mass and distance from the center of an object.

    Acceleration due to gravity on a planet depends on the planet's mass and radius; it varies directly with mass and proportionally to the inverse square of the radius (m/r^2). If this planet has the same mass as the Earth, its radius must be smaller so that the planet is denser than the earth. If the radius of the planet is the same as the Earth's, it must have a larger mass and density. However, we are not given any of this information, so the only thing we can say is that the value of m/r^2 for the planet is larger than the Earth's.

11. **b) 20 N**. This problem involves Newton's second law ($F = ma$). To find the force required, we must first calculate the desired acceleration, which is the rate of change of velocity,
    $a = \Delta v/\Delta t = 10/5 = 2$ m/s^2. Newton's second law states that $F = ma = 10 * 2 = 20$ N.

12. **a) 0 m/s**. The key to this question is that the object "begins at rest". In order for an object at rest to begin moving, the maximum static friction force must first be overcome, $F_{f,s} = \mu_s * N = 0.6 * 50 = 30$ N.

Since the force being applied is less than the "stiction" force, the object will not move. The force of friction in this case is equal to the 27 N being applied. Had the force been greater than 30 N, the object would move, a kinetic friction force of $F_{f,k} = \mu_k * N = 0.5 * 50 = 25$ N would resist the motion, and the speed at steady state would be much more difficult to find.

13. **b) Speed-multiplier**. Remember that in a gear train it is only necessary to look at the input and output gears. Since the input gear is larger than the output, the output gear will turn faster, making this a speed-multiplying gear train.

14. **c) The left side will go down and the right side will go up**. Air flowing through the duct will have to speed up at the narrow portion. According to Bernoulli's principle, the pressure in the air will decrease when the speed increases, so the pressure on the right side of the U-tube will be less than the pressure on the left side. This will push the water downward in the left side of the pipe and, since the volume of the water will stay constant (the water is incompressible), the water in the right side will rise.

15. **b) Torque-multiplier**. Pulley trains which include a wheel and axle like this one are not as simple as gear trains; you can't just look at the input and output pulleys. Instead, you have to look at each step of the pulleys. Fortunately, both steps of this system decrease the speed and increase torque, so this assembly is a torque-multiplier.

16. **b) Hold the scissors at D and cut at B**. For the best leverage, the input arm should be long and the output arm should be short. This means the load should be close to the fulcrum at B and the effort should be far from the fulcrum at D.

17. **b) Object 2**. Object 1 is farther away from the fulcrum, giving it a greater torque arm and therefore higher mechanical advantage that object 2. Since the lever is horizontal, the moments cause by the two objects must be equal, $F_1 R_1 = F_2 R_2$. $R_1 > R_2$, so therefore $F_2 > F_1$.

18. **b) Lower gears have a higher mechanical advantage**. When driving a car, the transmission is shifted into higher gears when the car is moving faster, so the higher gears are able to produce a higher speed at the expense of torque, meaning they have less of a mechanical advantage. If a person puts a manual transmission in a high gear and tries to move a car from rest, the engine speed will drop and the engine will most likely not have enough power to start because there is not enough of a mechanical advantage. This can also break the car's clutch.

19. a) Left supports more weight. The support on the left will carry more of the object's weight. Several approaches can be taken to analyze this problem.

If the support on the left is treated as a fulcrum and the support on the right as a force, similar to a class 2 lever, the force will not have to be large because it has a high mechanical advantage.

However, if the support on the right is treated as a fulcrum and the support on the left treated as an effort force, the force will not have much of a mechanical advantage.

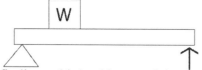

The question is analogous to finding which object weighs more on a balance, as shown below. The weight on the left represents the reaction force of the support on the left in the original question and the weight on the right represents the reaction force of the support on the right.

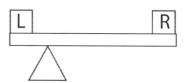

You can also think of the two extremes; if the weight is all the way to the left over the left support, the right support can be removed because it carries no load. Similarly, if the object is all the way on the right side, the right support carries the entire load. Since the object is closer to the left, the left support should carry more of the weight.

20. c) The silver cube. The speed at which the cubes will heat up depends on their thermal conductivity. Wood does not have a very high thermal conductivity. In metals, thermal conductivity generally follows the same trend as electrical conductivity; metals with high electrical conductivity have high thermal conductivity. This means the silver cube has the highest coefficient of thermal conductivity and will therefore heat the fastest.

21. B) II. Looking closely at the figure: the two pulleys above the weight in II are attached, and the weight in setup II has four rope segments extending from it, so the mechanical advantage is four and $F = W/4$. Setups I and III have two rope segments extending from the weight, giving a mechanical advantage of 2, and setup IV has three rope segments extending from it, so setup IV's mechanical advantage is 3.

22. b) Object 1 has the lowest density. How high an object floats in water depends on that object's density. The objects are acted on by the force of gravity, which depends on the objects mass and a buoyancy force that depends on the volume of the liquid displaced. If the question stated that the three objects had the same volume, then object 3 would be the

176

heaviest because it has the highest density and density is mass per unit volume. However, the problem does not state this and the height at which an object floats only gives its density.

23. a) 6 teeth. The pinion refers to the smaller of the two gears, so whether the mechanical advantage is 1:4 or 4:1, the pinion will have one quarter the number of teeth as the gear.

24. d) It is impossible to tell from this information. Though it is tempting to say object 2 weighs more, this hydraulic system gives the force applied to the piston on the right a mechanical advantage, so object 2 could actually weigh the same or less than object 1 and still push object 1 upward. Remember, the weight of object 1 is spread over a greater area, causing less pressure, while the weight of object 2 is concentrated on a smaller area and causes greater pressure.

25. d) 540 degrees. It is important to note first that the lower pulley attached to the crankshaft is rotating clockwise. This means that the camshaft is also rotating clockwise. The camshaft must turn 270 degrees (3/4 turn) before the cam is aligned with the valve stem so it is pushed as far down as it will go. The crankshaft turns at twice the speed of the camshaft, so it must rotate twice as far, 540 degrees (1.5 turns).

26. b) The spring will extend. This is a class three lever, where the weight is the load and the spring is the effort. If the weight is moved to the left, the load's torque arm is shortened and the weight has less leverage. This means the spring does not have to apply as much force and therefore expands.

27. c) Inclined plane. The axe in the picture is a wedge. Remember that a wedge is a type of inclined plane.

28. d) 4. The mechanical advantage of the lever is the length of the input arm divided by the length of the output arm (d_{in}/d_{out}), but the two lengths must be in the same units first. The input arm is two feet or 24 inches and the output arm is 6 inches, which is half a foot. Either way, $24/6 = 2/.5 = 4$

29. . Normally, it is only necessary to consider the input and output gears. However, in this gear train three consecutive gears are touching, which means that this gear train will not be able to turn since two consecutive gears should turn in opposite directions.

30. b) The pulley train on the right. The pulley system has a greater mechanical advantage. For the gear train, the mechanical advantage can be found from the diameters of the input and output gears. The pulley system has two steps, both of which are torque-multipliers. The pulley system's input and output pulleys may have the same diameter of the gear train's input and output gears, but the wheel and axle in the pulley system give it a greater mechanical advantage.

Made in the USA
Lexington, KY
07 October 2014